JANUARY 2020

PEACE TO PROSPERITY

A Vision to Improve the
Lives of the Palestinian
and Israeli People

Published by Diana Publishing

dianapublishing@yahoo.com

PART A

POLITICAL FRAMEWORK

CONTENTS

GLOSSARY

AL QUDS: Shall have the meaning set forth in Section 5

CONCEPTUAL MAP: Shall have the meaning set forth in Section 4

CROSSINGS BOARD: Shall have the meaning set forth in Section 8

GAZA CRITERIA: Shall have the meaning set forth in Section 9

IDF: Shall have the meaning set forth in Section 1

INTERNATIONAL FUND: Shall have the meaning set forth in Section 4

ISRAEL-JORDAN PEACE TREATY: shall mean the Treaty of Peace between the State of Israel and the Hashemite Kingdom of Jordan dated October 26, 1994.

ISRAELI-PALESTINIAN PEACE AGREEMENT: Shall have the meaning set forth in Section 3

JTDA: Shall have the meaning set forth in Section 5

MUSLIM HOLY SHRINES: Shall refer to the "Muslim Holy shrines" contemplated by the Israel-Jordan Peace Treaty.

OSCME: Shall have the meaning set forth in Section 19

PRISONER & MARTYR PAYMENTS: Shall have the meaning set forth in Section 23

PALESTINIAN REFUGEE TRUST: Shall have the meaning set forth in Section 16

PASF: Shall have the meaning set forth in Section 1

REVIEW COMMITTEE: Shall have the meaning set forth in Section 7

RSC: Shall have the meaning set forth in Section 7

SECURITY CRITERIA: Shall have the meaning set forth in Section 7

STATE OF PALESTINE: Throughout the Vision, the term "State of Palestine" refers to a future state, not currently in existence that could be recognized by the United States only if the criteria described in this Vision are satisfactorily met.

TRUMP ECONOMIC PLAN: Shall have the meaning set forth in Section 6

UNRWA: Shall mean the United Nations Relief and Works Agency

VISION: Shall have the meaning set forth in Section 1

INTRODUCTION[1]

BACKGROUND

Israelis and Palestinians have both suffered greatly from their long-standing and seemingly interminable conflict. For nearly a century, international leaders, diplomats, and scholars have debated the issues and attempted to resolve this conflict. The world has changed greatly during this period, as have the security challenges facing the Middle East. Many of the disputed issues have remained largely the same, and stubbornly intractable. The time has come to end the conflict, and unlock the vast human potential and economic opportunity that peace will bring to Israelis, Palestinians and the region as a whole. Over the decades, many proposals and ideas have been put forward, but elements of those plans were unachievable given the realities on the ground and in the broader Middle East. While no plan will give either side all of what it wants, what follows is our view of the best, most realistic and most achievable outcome for the parties.

Palestinians have aspirations that have not been realized, including self-determination, improvement of their standard of living, social betterment, and a respected place in the region, as well as among the nations of the world. Many Palestinians desire peace and recognize the enormous economic opportunities and social benefits that await them if relations with the State of Israel can be normalized. Gaza is a very complicated situation. It is under the control of Hamas, a terrorist organization, and, as a result of Hamas' policies, is approaching a humanitarian crisis. It is time to help the Palestinians achieve a hopeful and prosperous future and enable them to join the community of nations.

The State of Israel has made peace with two of its neighbors. It made peace with the Arab Republic of Egypt in 1979 and it made peace with the Hashemite Kingdom of Jordan in 1994, two countries with which the State of Israel had fought multiple wars and numerous border skirmishes. The State of Israel has also exchanged sizeable territories for the sake of peace, as it did when it withdrew from the Sinai Peninsula in exchange for peace with the Arab Republic of Egypt. While Israeli citizens have suffered greatly as a result of violence and terrorism, Israelis still desire peace. These two peace agreements, now 40 and 25 years old, have endured and bettered the lives of citizens in Israel, Jordan and Egypt.

The conflict between the State of Israel and the Palestinians has kept other Arab countries from normalizing their relationships and jointly pursuing a stable, secure, and prosperous region. One reason for the intractability of this problem is the conflation of two separate conflicts: a territorial, security and refugee dispute between Israel and the Palestinians and a religious dispute between Israel and the Muslim world regarding control over places of religious significance. The absence of formal relations between Israel and most Muslim and Arab countries has only exacerbated the conflict between Israelis and Palestinians. We believe that if more Muslim and Arab countries normalize relations with Israel it will help advance a just and fair resolution to the conflict between Israelis and Palestinians, and prevent radicals from using this conflict to destabilize the region.

---

[1] Capitalized terms used herein shall have the meaning ascribed to them in the Glossary.

OSLO

In 1993, the State of Israel and the Palestine Liberation Organization reached the first of several interim agreements, known collectively as the Oslo Accords.

Prime Minister Yitzchak Rabin, who signed the Oslo Accords and who in 1995 gave his life to the cause of peace, outlined in his last speech to the Israeli Knesset his vision regarding the ultimate resolution of the conflict. He envisioned Jerusalem remaining united under Israeli rule, the portions of the West Bank with large Jewish populations and the Jordan Valley being incorporated into Israel, and the remainder of the West Bank, along with Gaza, becoming subject to Palestinian civil autonomy in what he said would be something "less than a state." Rabin's vision was the basis upon which the Knesset approved the Oslo Accords, and it was not rejected by the Palestinian leadership at the time.

One of the most significant understandings within those agreements provided for security cooperation between the Israel Defense Forces (the "**IDF**") and the Palestinian Authority Security Forces (the "**PASF**"). While not perfect, and subject to periodic disputes and even suspension, the security cooperation in recent years has greatly enhanced the stability of the West Bank for both Palestinian and Israeli residents. The ability of the IDF and the PASF to work cooperatively together provides hope that security challenges can be bridged in a final Israeli-Palestinian Peace Agreement.

The Oslo Accords, however, left numerous key issues unresolved pending the completion of permanent status negotiations, including, among other items, borders, security, refugees and Jerusalem. Those agreements did not create an effective path for neutralizing the kinds of crises that emerged during the implementation of Oslo, including waves of terror and violence. Many intelligent and dedicated people have devoted lifetimes in search of the "ultimate deal," but what is required, a comprehensive agreement has been elusive, and waves of terror and violence have set back the process significantly. Only a comprehensive agreement, coupled with a strong economic plan for the Palestinians and others, has the capacity to bring lasting peace to the parties.

REALISTIC TWO-STATE SOLUTION

The principles set forth in this Vision for Peace, Prosperity and a Brighter Future (collectively, this "**VISION**"), are designed for the benefit of Palestinians, Israelis and the region as a whole. This Vision addresses today's realities, and provides the Palestinians, who do not yet have a state, with a path to a dignified national life, respect, security and economic opportunity and, at the same time, safeguards Israel's security.

A realistic solution would give the Palestinians all the power to govern themselves but not the powers to threaten Israel. This necessarily entails the limitations of certain sovereign powers in the Palestinian areas (henceforth referred to as the "Palestinian State") such as maintenance of Israeli security responsibility and Israeli control of the airspace west of the Jordan River. This Vision creates a realistic Two-State solution in which a secure and prosperous State of Palestine is living peacefully alongside a secure and prosperous State of Israel in a secure and prosperous region.

Today, that concept seems so far from reality. Gaza and the West Bank are politically divided. Gaza is run by Hamas, a terror organization that has fired thousands of rockets at Israel and murdered hundreds of Israelis. In the West Bank, the Palestinian Authority is plagued by failed institutions and endemic corruption. Its laws incentivize terrorism and Palestinian Authority controlled media and schools promote a culture of incitement. It is because of the lack of accountability and bad governance that billions of dollars have been squandered and investment is unable to flow into these areas to allow the Palestinians to thrive.

The Palestinians deserve a better future and this Vision can help them achieve that future. Palestinian leaders must embrace peace by recognizing Israel as the Jewish state, rejecting terrorism in all its forms, allowing for special arrangements that address Israel's and the region's vital security needs, building effective institutions and choosing pragmatic solutions. If these steps are taken and the criteria set forth in this Vision are satisfied, then the United States will support the establishment of a Palestinian State.

This Vision is security-focused, and provides both self-determination and significant economic opportunity for Palestinians. We believe that this design will enable this Vision to be successfully implemented. This Vision also provides positive benefits to the Hashemite Kingdom of Jordan, the Arab Republic of Egypt and countries throughout the region.

OPPORTUNITIES FOR REGIONAL COOPERATION

The Middle East has gone through dramatic shifts since the beginning of this conflict. In confronting common threats and in pursuing common interests, previously unimaginable opportunities and alliances are emerging. The threats posed by Iran's radical regime for example, have led to a new reality, where the State of Israel and its Arab neighbors now share increasingly similar perceptions of the threats to their security. If peace can be achieved, the economic and security cooperation between the State of Israel and its Arab neighbors can create a prosperous Middle East that is connected by a common desire for security and economic opportunity. If implemented, this Vision can lead to direct flights between the State of Israel and its neighbors, the transport of people and commerce and the unlocking of opportunities for millions of people to visit religious sites sacred to their faiths.

ECONOMIC VISION FOR A PROSPEROUS FUTURE

We developed a detailed economic vision for what the future for the Palestinians could be if there were peace. There has been a false notion that the lack of opportunity for the Palestinian people is Israel's sole responsibility. Solving the final status issues, in the manner described in this Vision, would create the necessary conditions for investment to start flowing into the region. We estimate that combining this political solution with the economic vision for investments and government reforms that we have laid out will lead to historic economic growth. We estimate that the Palestinian GDP, which has been stagnant, could double in 10 years, create over 1 million new jobs, reduce the unemployment rate below 10 percent, and reduce the poverty rate by 50 percent. This plan is ready to be implemented in the event that peace can be made on terms consistent with this Vision.

THE APPROACH

We do not believe that the parties in the region are fated to live in eternal conflict because of their different ethnicities and faiths. There have been many examples in history of Jews and Arabs, and Jews and Muslims and Christians, living in relative harmony in this region. Our hope is that this Vision inspires a future in which all the peoples in the region live together in peace and prosperity.

We have developed this Vision based on the belief that a peaceful and prosperous future can exist for Palestinians and Israelis alike. This Vision is intended for people to read, understand and imagine how its concepts will actually and dramatically improve their lives. We believe that both sides gain more than they give. Based on this approach, we encourage all to be intellectually honest, open to new ideas, willing to engage on this Vision and take courageous steps toward a better future for themselves and for future generations.

Learning from past efforts, and driven by pragmatic principles, we approach this conflict guided by the following points:

OVERVIEW OF UNITED NATIONS EFFORTS

> Since 1946, there have been close to 700 United Nations General Assembly resolutions and over 100 United Nations Security Council resolutions in connection with this conflict. United Nations resolutions are sometimes inconsistent and sometimes time-bound. These resolutions have not brought about peace. Furthermore, different parties have offered conflicting interpretations of some of the most significant United Nations resolutions, including United Nations Security Council Resolution 242. Indeed, legal scholars who have worked directly on critical United Nations resolutions have differed on their meaning and legal effect.

> While we are respectful of the historic role of the United Nations in the peace process, this Vision is not a recitation of General Assembly, Security Council and other international resolutions on this topic because such resolutions have not and will not resolve the conflict. For too long these resolutions have enabled political leaders to avoid addressing the complexities of this conflict rather than enabling a realistic path to peace.

CURRENT REALITIES

> Both Israelis and Palestinians have long-standing negotiating positions but also must recognize that compromise is necessary to move forward. It is inevitable that each side will support and oppose aspects of this Vision. It is essential that this Vision be assessed holistically. This Vision presents a package of compromises that both sides should consider, in order to move forward and pursue a better future that will benefit both of them and others in the region.

- A peace agreement will be forged only when each side recognizes that it is better off with a peace agreement than without one, even one that requires difficult compromises. Peace between Israelis and Palestinians will lead to significant social and economic improvements, stability, and security for Israelis and Palestinians alike.

- There are those who benefit from the status quo and, accordingly, seek to prevent change that would benefit both parties.

- Reciting past narratives about the conflict is unproductive. In order to resolve this conflict, the solution must be forward-looking and dedicated to the improvement of security and quality of life, while being respectful of the historic and religious significance of the region to its peoples.

- Limited framework agreements and vague proposals, which are heavily wordsmithed and include only high-level concepts, but leave the disagreements to be resolved later, have not worked. This Vision directly addresses all major issues in an attempt to genuinely resolve the conflict.

- Solving this conflict will not solve all the other conflicts in the region. However, resolving the Israeli-Palestinian conflict will remove a pretext used to stoke emotion and justify radical behavior by bad actors and have a positive impact that will increase stability, security and prosperity in the region.

- The Israeli-Palestinian Peace Agreement will deeply and profoundly impact Israelis and Palestinians. It is the Israelis and Palestinians who will have to live with the consequences of a peace agreement. Therefore, it is Israelis and Palestinians themselves, who must be satisfied with the benefits and compromises that a peace agreement entails. Israelis and Palestinians must weigh those benefits and compromises, which can create a far better future for themselves and future generations, against the continuation of the conflict for perhaps generations to come.

- The role of the United States as facilitator in this process has been to collect ideas from around the world, compile them, and propose a detailed set of recommendations that can realistically and appropriately solve the conflict. The role of the United States is also to work together with other well-meaning countries and organizations to assist the parties in reaching a resolution to the conflict. But only the Israelis and Palestinians themselves can make the decision to forge a lasting peace together. The final, specific details of the Israeli-Palestinian Peace Agreement, must be worked out directly between the parties.

- A main fault line in the Middle East today is between leaders who want to create economic opportunity and a better life for their peoples, and those who manipulate religion and ideology in order to foment conflict and excuse their failures. This Vision aims to be respectful of ideology, religious beliefs and historical claims, but is focused primarily on putting the interests and aspirations of the people first.

- We have entered a new chapter in the Middle East's history, in which courageous leaders understand that new and shared threats have created the need for greater regional cooperation. The Trump Administration has strongly encouraged this.

> Arab countries in the region have been held hostage to this conflict and recognize that it represents an uncapped financial liability to them if it remains unresolved. Many Arab countries are ready to resolve the Arab-Israeli conflict and want to partner with Israel and focus on the serious issues facing the region.

LEGITIMATE ASPIRATIONS OF THE PARTIES

> While the Palestinians have never had a state, they have a legitimate desire to rule themselves and chart their own destiny. Any workable peace agreement must address the Palestinians' legitimate desire for self-determination. This Vision addresses these legitimate concerns through, among other things, the designation of territory for a future Palestinian state, strengthening Palestinian institutions of self-government, providing Palestinians with the legal status and international standing of a state, ensuring solid security arrangements, and building an innovative network of roads, bridges and tunnels that enables freedom of movement for the Palestinians.

> The State of Israel has a legitimate desire to be the nation-state of the Jewish people and for that status to be recognized throughout the world.

> This Vision aims to achieve mutual recognition of the State of Israel as the nation state of the Jewish people, and the State of Palestine as the nation-state of the Palestinian people, in each case with equal civil rights for all citizens within each state.

> This Vision aims to achieve the recognition by, and normalization with, those countries who do not currently recognize the State of Israel or have a relationship with the State of Israel.

> This Vision aims to achieve the recognition by, and normalization with, those countries that do not currently recognize the State of Palestine or have a relationship with the Palestinians.

THE PRIMACY OF SECURITY

> Even if a comprehensive peace agreement is achieved between the State of Israel, the State of Palestine and additional Arab states, the reality is that there will always exist those who desire to undermine security and stability. This Vision always keeps this reality in mind.

> No government should be asked to compromise the safety and security of its citizens. This is especially true for the State of Israel, a country that since its establishment has faced, and continues to face, enemies that call for its annihilation. Israel has also had the bitter experience of withdrawing from territories that were then used to launch attacks against it.

> The State of Israel suffers from extraordinary geographic and geostrategic challenges. Simply put, the State of Israel has no margin for error. As dangerous as Gaza, run by Hamas, is to the State of Israel's safety, a similar regime

controlling the West Bank would pose an existential threat to the State of Israel.

> It is essential that a Palestinian state created under a peace deal be a state that has the tools to succeed and that it is peaceful and secure, rather than a platform for instability and conflict.

> The United States cannot ask any country, let alone the State of Israel, a close ally, to make compromises that would exacerbate an already precarious security situation. The United States would only ask Israel to make compromises that we believe will make the State of Israel and the people of Israel more secure in the short and long term. This Vision was designed in that spirit. All other countries should take the same approach.

> The threat of terrorism has spread worldwide. Today, governments closely coordinate with one another to leverage their intelligence expertise to fight terrorism. It is important that governments unambiguously condemn all forms of terrorism, and that governments work together to fight against global terrorism.

> Both Israelis and Palestinians (as well as the surrounding region) benefit greatly from enhanced security. The protection of Palestinians also protects Israelis, and similarly the protection of Israelis also protects Palestinians.

> Counterterrorism cooperation between the State of Israel, the Hashemite Kingdom of Jordan, the Arab Republic of Egypt and others in the region has enhanced the security of each of these states. This Vision is based upon the belief that cooperation between the State of Israel and the State of Palestine will also benefit both states. Existing coordination between the Israelis and Palestinians provides hope that this can be achieved.

> This Vision has been developed in a manner that takes into account the security needs of, and future strategic threats to, Israelis, Palestinians and the region.

THE QUESTION OF TERRITORY, SELF-DETERMINATION AND SOVEREIGNTY

> Any realistic peace proposal requires the State of Israel to make a significant territorial compromise that will enable the Palestinians to have a viable state, respect their dignity and address their legitimate national aspirations.

> Withdrawing from territory captured in a defensive war is a historical rarity. It must be recognized that the State of Israel has already withdrawn from at least 88% of the territory it captured in 1967. This Vision provides for the transfer of sizeable territory by the State of Israel -- territory to which Israel has asserted valid legal and historical claims, and which are part of the ancestral homeland of the Jewish people -- which must be considered a significant concession.

> Peace should not demand the uprooting of people – Arab or Jew – from their homes. Such a construct, which is more likely to lead to civil unrest, runs counter to the idea of co-existence.

> Transportation corridors included in this Vision create transportation contiguity that greatly reduces the need for checkpoints and greatly enhances the mobility and quality of life and commerce for the Palestinian people.

> Self-determination is the hallmark of a nation. This Vision is intended to maximize self-determination, while taking all relevant factors into account.

> Sovereignty is an amorphous concept that has evolved over time. With growing interdependence, each nation chooses to interact with other nations by entering into agreements that set parameters essential to each nation. The notion that sovereignty is a static and consistently defined term has been an unnecessary stumbling block in past negotiations. Pragmatic and operational concerns that effect security and prosperity are what is most important.

REFUGEES

> The international community is struggling to find sufficient funds to address the needs of the over 70 million refugees and displaced persons in the world today. In 2020 alone, the United Nations has asked for over $8.5 billion in new funding to help the millions of Syrian refugees and others around the world. Most of those refugees were expelled or fled from their homes in the recent past and face dire circumstances.

> The Arab-Israeli conflict created both a Palestinian and Jewish refugee problem.

> Palestinian refugees, who have suffered over the past 70 years, have been treated as pawns on the broader Middle East chessboard, and empty promises have been made to them and to their host countries. A just, fair and realistic solution to the Palestinian refugee issue is necessary to resolve the Israeli-Palestinian conflict.

> A similar number of Jewish refugees were expelled from Arab lands shortly after the creation of the State of Israel, and have also suffered. A just solution for these Jewish refugees should be implemented through an appropriate international mechanism separate from the Israel-Palestinian Peace Agreement.

JERUSALEM

> Jerusalem is holy to multiple faiths and has religious significance for much of humanity.

> The issue of Jerusalem's holy sites, particularly the Temple Mount/Haram al-Sharif should be treated with the utmost sensitivity.

> The State of Israel has been a good custodian of Jerusalem. During Israel's stewardship, it has kept Jerusalem open and secure.

> Jerusalem should be a city that unites people and should always remain open to worshippers of all religions.

THE PROBLEM OF GAZA

> Gaza has tremendous potential but is currently held hostage by Hamas, Palestinian Islamic Jihad (PIJ) and other terrorist organizations committed to Israel's destruction. The terrorist organizations running Gaza have not improved the lives of the people living there. As these groups have gained power and increased their malign activity, the suffering of the people of Gaza has only increased.

> Israel has tightened security over Gaza in order to prevent weapons, and materials that are used to make weapons, from entering. Any acceptable solution must allow goods to pass through so that the Gaza economy can thrive while making sure Israel's legitimate security concerns are addressed.

> The United States does not expect the State of Israel to negotiate with any Palestinian government that includes any members of Hamas, PIJ or surrogates thereof, unless that Palestinian government (including its members from Hamas or PIJ) unambiguously and explicitly commit to nonviolence, recognize the State of Israel, and fully satisfy the other Gaza Criteria, set forth in Section 9.

> Should negotiations between Israelis and Palestinians result in a peace agreement, the State of Israel will be expected to implement its obligations under the Israeli-Palestinian Peace Agreement only if the Palestinian Authority, or another body acceptable to Israel, has full control of Gaza, terror organizations in Gaza are disarmed, and Gaza is fully demilitarized.

> For comprehensive peace to be achieved, it is up to the Palestinian people to make clear that they reject the ideologies of destruction, terror and conflict, and unite for a better future for all Palestinians.

INTERNATIONAL ASSISTANCE

> Countries that have donated funds to the Palestinians over the course of the conflict all have other significant challenges and needs and want to ensure that aid to the Palestinians will be spent wisely and significantly reduced over time. This Vision has been developed to reduce over time the Palestinians' dependence on aid from the international community. The goal of the Israeli-Palestinian Peace Agreement is a thriving Palestinian economy and a viable state.

SECTION THREE

A VISION FOR PEACE BETWEEN THE STATE OF ISRAEL, THE PALESTINIANS AND THE REGION

The conflict has grown old, the arguments have become worn, and the parties have failed to achieve peace. At this point, only a comprehensive answer to the critical issues has the potential to galvanize the parties to end this seemingly intractable conflict. Both parties must make significant and difficult compromises to achieve greater gains.

The peace agreement that will hopefully be negotiated on the basis of this Vision should be implemented through legally binding contracts and agreements (the "**ISRAELI-PALESTINIAN PEACE AGREEMENT**").

It is also the hope of the United States that Arab nations within the region that have yet to achieve peace with the State of Israel will immediately begin to normalize relations with Israel and eventually negotiate peace agreements with Israel.

Each appendix attached to this Vision is an integral part of this Vision.

SECTION FOUR

BORDERS

A conceptual map (the "**CONCEPTUAL MAP**") is attached hereto based on the guiding principles set forward in this Vision.

The Conceptual Map has been designed to demonstrate the feasibility for a redrawing of boundaries in the spirit of UNSCR 242, and in a manner that:

1. Meets the security requirements of the State of Israel;

2. Delivers significant territorial expansion to the Palestinians;

3. Takes into account the State of Israel's valid legal and historical claims;

4. Avoids forced population transfers of either Arab or Jews;

5. Enhances mobility for both Israelis and Palestinians within their respective states;

6. Provides pragmatic transportation solutions to address the needs of the Israeli and Palestinian enclaves that are described below;

7. Enhances the commercial viability and economic independence of the State of Palestine,

8. Provides for a potentially significant expansion of Gaza to enhance its development and success; and

9. Facilitates the integration of the State of Palestine into the regional and global economy.

The State of Israel and the United States do not believe the State of Israel is legally bound to provide the Palestinians with

100 percent of pre-1967 territory (a belief that is consistent with United Nations Security Council Resolution 242). This Vision is a fair compromise, and contemplates a Palestinian state that encompasses territory reasonably comparable in size to the territory of the West Bank and Gaza pre-1967.

This Vision also contemplates a Palestinian state that maximizes ease of travel within the State of Palestine through state-of-the-art infrastructure solutions comprised of bridges, roads and tunnels, and provides significant benefits well beyond the borders of the State of Palestine. For example, the State of Palestine will benefit from a high-speed transportation link that will enable efficient movement between the West Bank and Gaza, crossing over or under the State of Israel's sovereign territory. This crossing, which didn't exist before 1967, will greatly enhance the value of the Israeli-Palestinian Peace Agreement for the Palestinians, and will be designed to be a part of a new regional infrastructure linking Palestinians and Israelis to the broader Middle East, as described below.

Moreover, until such time as the State of Palestine may develop its own port (as described below), the State of Palestine will benefit from special access to certain designated facilities at the State of Israel's Haifa and Ashdod ports, with an efficient means of exporting and importing goods into and out of the State of Palestine without compromising Israel's security.

The State of Israel will benefit from having secure and recognized borders. It will not have to uproot any settlements, and will incorporate the vast majority of Israeli settlements into contiguous Israeli territory. Israeli enclaves located inside contiguous Palestinian territory will become part of the State of Israel and be connected to it through an effective transportation system.

The United States has designed the Conceptual Map to include the following features:

> Approximately 97% of Israelis in the West Bank will be incorporated into contiguous Israeli territory, and approximately 97% of Palestinians in the West Bank will be incorporated into contiguous Palestinian territory. Land swaps will provide the State of Palestine with land reasonably comparable in size to the territory of pre-1967 West Bank and Gaza.

> The Palestinian population located in enclaves that remain inside contiguous Israeli territory but that are part of the State of Palestine shall become citizens of the State of Palestine and shall have the option to remain in place unless they choose otherwise. They will have access routes connecting them to the State of Palestine. They will be subject to Palestinian civilian administration, including zoning and planning, within the interior of such Palestinian enclaves. They will not be discriminated against and will have appropriate security protection. Such enclaves and access routes will be subject to Israeli security responsibility.

> The Israeli population located in enclaves that remain inside contiguous Palestinian territory but that are part of the State of Israel shall have the option to remain in place unless they choose otherwise, and maintain their existing Israeli citizenship. They will have access routes connecting them to the State of Israel. They will be subject to Israeli civilian administration, including zoning and planning, within the interior of such Israeli enclaves. They will not be discriminated against and will have appropriate security protection. Such enclaves and access routes will be subject to Israeli security responsibility.

> The Jordan Valley, which is critical for Israel's national security, will be under Israeli sovereignty. Notwithstanding such sovereignty, Israel should work with the Palestinian government to negotiate an agreement in which existing agricultural enterprises owned or controlled by Palestinians shall continue without interruption or discrimination, pursuant to appropriate licenses or leases granted by the State of Israel.

> For over a decade, Gaza has been ruled by Hamas, a terror organization, responsible for the murder and maiming of thousands of Israelis. Rather than dedicate themselves to improving the lives of the people of Gaza, Hamas, PIJ and other terror organizations have been dedicated to the destruction of Israel. At the same time, they have brutally repressed Palestinians and diverted hundreds of millions of dollars meant to improve Palestinian lives to fueling a war machine of thousands of rockets and missiles, dozens of terror tunnels and other lethal capabilities. As a result of Hamas' terror and misrule, the people of Gaza suffer from massive unemployment, widespread poverty, drastic shortages of electricity and potable water, and other problems that threaten to precipitate a wholesale humanitarian crisis. This Vision is designed to give Palestinians in Gaza a prosperous future. It provides for the possibility of allocating for the Palestinians Israeli territory close to Gaza (as depicted on the conceptual map) within which infrastructure may be rapidly built to address Gaza's pressing humanitarian needs, and which will eventually enable the building of thriving Palestinian cities and towns that will help the people of Gaza flourish.

> Significant improvements for the people in Gaza will not occur until there is a ceasefire with Israel, the full demilitarization of Gaza, and a governance structure that allows the international community to safely and comfortably put new money into investments that will not be destroyed by predictable future conflicts.

> The State of Israel will retain sovereignty over territorial waters, which are vital to Israel's security and which provides stability to the region.

> Land swaps provided by the State of Israel could include both populated and unpopulated areas.

> The Triangle Communities consist of Kafr Qara, Ar'ara, Baha al-Gharbiyye, Umm al Fahm, Qalansawe, Tayibe, Kafr Qasim, Tira, Kafr Bara and Jaljulia. These communities, which largely self-identify as Palestinian, were originally designated to fall under Jordanian control during the negotiations of the Armistice Line of 1949, but ultimately were retained by Israel for military reasons that have since been mitigated. The Vision contemplates the possibility, subject to agreement of the parties that the borders of Israel will be redrawn such that the Triangle Communities become part of the State of Palestine. In this agreement, the civil rights of the residents of the triangle communities would be subject to the applicable laws and judicial rulings of the relevant authorities.

> Beyond its borders, the State of Palestine will have high-speed transportation links (such as the West Bank/Gaza connection), and until such time as the State of Palestine may develop its own port, access to two designated port facilities in the State of Israel.

> Two access roads will be built for the benefit of the State of Palestine that will be subject to Israeli security requirements. These roads will enable Palestinians to cross the Jordan Valley to the border crossing with the

Hashemite Kingdom of Jordan, thereby facilitating Palestinian travel to and from the Hashemite Kingdom of Jordan and beyond, and subject to the immigration rules of the State of Palestine, allow Jordanians and others from the region to enter the State of Palestine.

> First-rate infrastructure solutions (including tunnels and overpasses) will be built to maximize unimpeded movement throughout both states and in between states and their respective enclaves.

> The security barrier will be realigned to match the new borders. New, modern and efficient border crossings will be constructed.

> The drawing of borders pursuant to the Conceptual Map shall be without prejudice to individual claims of title or rights of possession traditionally litigated within the Israeli judicial system.

> Freedom of access to all religious sites of all faiths in both states should be agreed to and respected by the parties. The State of Israel and the State of Palestine should enter into an access agreement to ensure freedom of access to and prayer rights at all religious sites within the State of Palestine and the State of Israel. A list of such holy sites should be compiled during negotiations between the parties.

> This Vision contemplates the establishment of an international fund (the "**INTERNATIONAL FUND**") for the development of the land swap areas designated for the State of Palestine, as well as all infrastructure improvements and all security measures contemplated by the Israeli-Palestinian Peace Agreement, including port facilities, roads, bridges, tunnels, fences, overpasses, rail links, border crossings and the like. The cost of these improvements and measures is not expected to be absorbed by the State of Israel or the State of Palestine.

SECTION FIVE

JERUSALEM

The United States recognizes the heightened sensitivity surrounding Jerusalem, a city that means so much to so many.

Jerusalem is a city unique in the history of civilization. No other place on earth can claim significance to three major religions. Each day, Jews pray at the Western Wall, Muslims bow in prayer at the al-Aqsa Mosque and Christians worship at the Church of the Holy Sepulchre.

Throughout history, Jerusalem has been subject to war and conquest. It has been used to divide people and to instigate conflict by those with evil intentions. But it does not have to be this way.

Jerusalem must remain a city that brings people of all faiths together to visit, to worship, to respect each other and to appreciate the majesty of history and the glory of God's creation.

The approach of this Vision is to keep Jerusalem united, make it accessible to all and to acknowledge its holiness to all in a manner that is respectful to all.

RELIGIOUS ASPECTS OF THE JERUSALEM ISSUE

We understand that theological interpretations differ within each religion. The descriptions below of Judaism, Christianity, and Islam are not intended to be definitive theological interpretations. It is nevertheless clear that each of these three great faiths has its own connection to Jerusalem.

For Judaism, Jerusalem is where Mount Moriah is located. According to Jewish tradition, it was there that Abraham nearly sacrificed his son, Isaac, until God intervened. Centuries later, Jerusalem became the political center of the Jewish people when King David united the twelve tribes of Israel, making the city the capital and spiritual center of the Jewish people, which it has remained for nearly 3,000 years. King David's son, King Solomon, built the First Temple on Mount Moriah. According to Jewish tradition, inside the Temple, within the Holy of Holies, were stored the original Ten Commandments, revealed by God to Moses at Mount Sinai. The First Temple was destroyed by the Babylonians in 586 B.C. The Second Temple was built atop the same mountain and stood until it was destroyed by the Romans in 70 A.D. However, Jerusalem never lost its holiness to the Jewish People: It remains the direction to which Jews throughout the world turn in prayer and the destination of Jewish pilgrimage. Every year, on the 9th day of the Jewish month of Av, Jews fast, mourn and commemorate the destruction of the two Temples. Although Jews pray today at the Western Wall, which was a retaining wall of the Second Temple, the Temple Mount itself is the holiest site in Judaism. There are nearly 700 separate references to Jerusalem in the Hebrew Bible. For 100 generations the hopes and dreams of the Jewish people have been encapsulated by the words "Next Year in Jerusalem."

For Christianity, Jerusalem is where Jesus of Nazareth preached, was tried, crucified, resurrected, and ascended to Heaven. Immediately after the recognition of Christianity as the official religion of the Roman Empire by Constantine in the early 4th century, religious institutions were established at important sites such as the Church of the Holy Sepulchre and the Mount of Olives. After the Islamic conquest of Jerusalem in 637, Christians longed to recover the holy city, which they finally achieved in 1099, although it was lost to them again in 1187. During the medieval period, Jerusalem remained the premier Christian pilgrimage site, and a steady stream of visitors followed the footsteps of Jesus through Jerusalem, despite the dangers and challenges inherent in such travel. Under the Ottoman Empire, Christians were granted legal rights to their holy sites by successive *firmans* in the 18th and 19th centuries, establishing the Christian "Status Quo," which was re-affirmed in the 1993 Vatican-Israel Fundamental Agreement. Today, Jerusalem is home to more than a dozen Christian sects and a thriving Christian population.

For Islam, Jerusalem acquires prominence as stated in the Holy Koran: "Glory to Him who made His Servant go by night from the Sacred Mosque (al-Masjid al-Haram) to the Farthest Mosque (al-Masjid al-Aqsa) whose surroundings We have blessed, that We might show him some of Our signs." According to Islamic tradition, the verse refers to the Prophet Muhammad's nocturnal journey from Mecca to Jerusalem (al-Isra'); he arrives at the area of the Temple Mount/Haram al-Sharif, where he ascends to Heaven (al-Mi'raj), to meet the earlier prophets and receive the commandment of prayer. In early Islam, when

Muhammad had taken his followers from Mecca to Medina, he established Jerusalem as the direction of Islamic prayer (the first Qiblah) before later changing the direction of prayer to Mecca. There have been Muslim rulers who also emphasized the religious importance of Jerusalem. The Ummayad Caliphate, based in Damascus, offered Jerusalem as an alternative place of pilgrimage when Mecca was controlled by a rival caliphate. The victory of Saladin over the Crusaders in 1187 led to a revival of Islamic interest in Jerusalem, and in 1517, Sultan Suleiman the Magnificent rebuilt its walls and religious sites. Today, it is widely considered the third holiest site in Islam.

JERUSALEM'S HOLY SITES

After the Six Day War in 1967, when the State of Israel took control over all of Jerusalem, the State of Israel assumed responsibility for protecting all of the city's holy sites. Those holy sites include, without limitation, the Temple Mount/Haram al-Sharif, the Western Wall, the Muslim Holy Shrines, Church of St. Anne, Via Dolorosa (Stations of the Cross), Church of the Holy Sepulchre, Church of Viri Galilaei, Church of St. Stephen, Dormition Abbey, Tomb of the Virgin Mary, Room of the Last Supper, Augusta Victoria Church of Ascension, Garden of Gethsemane, Church of Mary Magdalene, Dominus Flevit Church, Pater Noster Church, Church of St. Peter in Gallicantu, Church of the Ascension, The Russian Church, Secours Catholique 'House of Abraham,' Mount Scopus, Hurva Synagogue, Tomb of Absalom, Tomb of Zechariah, Second Temple Pilgrimage Road, Tomb of the Prophets Haggai, Zechariah and Malachi, Gihon Spring, City of David, Mount of Olives, Sambuski Jewish Cemetery, and the Pool of Siloam.

Unlike many previous powers that had ruled Jerusalem, and had destroyed the holy sites of other faiths, the State of Israel is to be commended for safeguarding the religious sites of all and maintaining a religious status quo.

Given this commendable record for more than half a century, as well as the extreme sensitivity regarding some of Jerusalem's holy sites, we believe that this practice should remain, and that all of Jerusalem's holy sites should be subject to the same governance regimes that exist today. In particular the status quo at the Temple Mount/Haram al-Sharif should continue uninterrupted.

Jerusalem's holy sites should remain open and available for peaceful worshippers and tourists of all faiths. People of every faith should be permitted to pray on the Temple Mount/Haram al-Sharif, in a manner that is fully respectful to their religion, taking into account the times of each religion's prayers and holidays, as well as other religious factors.

POLITICAL STATUS OF JERUSALEM

One of the most complicated issues in achieving peace is resolving the question of the political status of Jerusalem.

Prior to 1967, a divided Jerusalem was a source of great tension in the region, with Jordanian and Israeli forces separated by barbed wire and Israeli residents of Jerusalem endangered by sniper fire.

A division of Jerusalem would be inconsistent with the policy statements of the Jerusalem Embassy Act of 1995 of the United States. All former presidents who have been involved in the peace process have agreed that Jerusalem should not be physically divided again.

On December 6, 2017, on behalf of the United States of America, President Trump recognized Jerusalem as Israel's capital. The President also made clear that the specific boundaries of Israeli sovereignty in Jerusalem would be subject to final status negotiations between the parties.

We believe that returning to a divided Jerusalem, and in particular having two separate security forces in one of the most sensitive areas on earth, would be a grave mistake.

While a physical division of the city must be avoided, a security barrier currently exists that does not follow the municipal boundary and that already separates Arab neighborhoods (i.e., Kafr Aqab, and the eastern part of Shuafat) in Jerusalem from the rest of the neighborhoods in the city.

This physical barrier should remain in place and should serve as a border between the capitals of the two parties.

Jerusalem will remain the sovereign capital of the State of Israel, and it should remain an undivided city. The sovereign capital of the State of Palestine should be in the section of East Jerusalem located in all areas east and north of the existing security barrier, including Kafr Aqab, the eastern part of Shuafat and Abu Dis, and could be named Al Quds or another name as determined by the State of Palestine.

This Vision would allow the Arab residents of Israel's capital, Jerusalem, beyond the 1949 armistice lines but inside the existing security barrier to choose one of three options:

1. Become citizens of the State of Israel

2. Become citizens of the State of Palestine

3. Retain their status as permanent residents in Israel.

Over the years, some Arab residents of these areas (approximately 6%) have chosen to become Israeli citizens, and that option should remain available to Arab residents of these areas in the future.

Other Arab residents of these areas may want to embrace a Palestinian political identity by choosing to become citizens of the State of Palestine, and that option should be available to them as well.

Many of the Arab residents of these areas may want to maintain a political identity that is separate from either Israel or Palestine, and which allows them to take pride in their unique identity and history. That option should remain available to them.

PRIVILEGES, BENEFITS AND OBLIGATIONS

The privileges, benefits and obligations of Arab residents of these areas who choose to keep their status as permanent residents of Israel should remain the same.

The privileges, benefits and obligations of Arab residents of these areas who choose to become citizens of Palestine will be determined by the laws of the State of Palestine and the State of Israel, as applicable.

The residents of these areas who choose to become citizens of the State of Israel will have all the privileges, benefits and obligations of being citizens of the State of Israel. Residents of these areas, who today are citizens of Israel, will maintain the same privileges, benefits and obligations that they have today.

SPECIAL TOURIST AREA

The State of Israel should allow for the development by the State of Palestine of a special tourism zone in Atarot, in a specific area to be agreed upon by the parties. We envision that this area should be a world class tourist zone that should support Muslim tourism to Jerusalem and its holy sites. We envision that this zone will become a thriving and vibrant tourism center that includes state-of-the-art public transportation that provides easy access to and from the holy sites.

To support this new development, the economic development program will identify financing for the construction of restaurants, shops, hotels, cultural centers, and other tourism facilities within this zone. Fast-track accessibility to the Muslim Holy Shrines should be developed and maintained. The specific details of this area, including, without limitation, taxation, and zoning should be negotiated between the parties.

TOURISM MATTERS RELATING TO THE OLD CITY OF JERUSALEM

Without derogating the State of Israel's sovereignty, during the negotiation of the Israeli-Palestinian Peace Agreement, and subject to the State of Israel's security requirements, the parties shall:

1. Negotiate a mechanism by which licenses shall be provided to Palestinian tour guides to operate tours in the Old City of Jerusalem as well as at sites sacred to Christianity and Islam in other areas of Jerusalem;

2. Establish a Jerusalem-Al Quds Joint Tourism Development Authority (the "**JTDA**"). The JTDA will work to promote Jewish, Muslim and Christian tourism in both the State of Israel and the State of Palestine. Israel will establish a mechanism whereby part of the tax revenues from the increased tourism in the Old City of Jerusalem will be allocated to the JTDA for further reinvestment for tourism in the Old City of Jerusalem. The JTDA will also work with the Hashemite Kingdom of Jordan to promote regional tourism.

RECOGNITION OF CAPITALS

Jerusalem should be internationally recognized as the capital of the State of Israel. Al Quds (or another name selected by the State of Palestine) should be internationally recognized as the capital of the State of Palestine.

Neither party shall encourage or support efforts by other countries or persons to deny the legitimacy of the other party's capital or its sovereignty. The mayors for each capital city will establish mechanisms for regular consultation and voluntary cooperation on matters of significance to the two capitals.

The embassy of the United States to the State of Israel will remain in Jerusalem. Following the signing of the Israeli-Palestinian Peace Agreement, the embassy of the United States to the State of Palestine will be in Al Quds at a location to be chosen by the United States, in agreement with the State of Palestine. The United States will recognize the State of Israel and the State of Palestine in their respective capitals and encourage other nations to relocate their embassies to Jerusalem and Al Quds, as applicable.

SECTION SIX
THE TRUMP ECONOMIC PLAN

At the invitation of the Kingdom of Bahrain, this past June in Manama, the United States presented the administration's Middle East Peace Economic Plan titled *Peace to Prosperity: A New Vision for the Palestinian People*.

The United States recognizes that the successful signing and implementation of the Israeli-Palestinian Peace Agreement will have a significant impact on the economic prospects of the region. In Bahrain, the international community stressed its commitment to the economic plan and its necessity, as well as its viability following the signing of a peace agreement.

The economic plan will empower the Palestinian people to build a prosperous and vibrant Palestinian society. It consists of three initiatives that will support distinct pillars of the Palestinian society: the economy, the people, and the government. With the potential to facilitate more than $50 billion in new investment over ten years, *Peace to Prosperity* represents the most ambitious and comprehensive international effort for the Palestinian people to date. It has the ability to fundamentally transform the West Bank and Gaza and to open a new chapter in Palestinian history, one defined, not by adversity and loss, but by opportunity and dignity.

The first initiative will unleash the economic potential of the Palestinian people. By developing property and contract rights, the rule of law, anti-corruption measures, capital markets, a pro-growth tax structure, and a low-tariff scheme with reduced trade barriers, this initiative envisions policy reforms coupled with strategic infrastructure investments that will improve the business environment and stimulate private-sector growth. Hospitals, schools, homes, and businesses will secure reliable access to affordable electricity, clean water, and digital services. Billions of dollars of new investment will flow into various sectors of the Palestinian economy. Businesses will have increased access to capital, and the markets of the West Bank and

Gaza will be connected with key trading partners, including Egypt, Israel, Jordan, and Lebanon. The resulting economic growth has the potential to end the current unemployment crisis and transform the West Bank and Gaza into a center of opportunity.

The second initiative will empower the Palestinian people to realize their ambitions. Through new data-driven, outcomes-based education options at home, expanded online education platforms, increased vocational and technical training, and the prospect of international exchanges, this initiative will enhance and expand a variety of programs that directly improve the well-being of the Palestinian people. It will strengthen the Palestinian educational system and ensure that students can fulfill their academic goals and be prepared for the workforce.

Equally important, access to quality healthcare will be dramatically improved, as Palestinian hospitals and clinics will be outfitted with the latest healthcare technology and equipment. In addition, new opportunities for cultural and recreational activities will improve the quality of life of the Palestinian people. From parks and cultural institutions to athletic facilities and libraries, this initiative's projects will enrich public life throughout the West Bank and Gaza.

The third initiative will enhance Palestinian governance, improving the public sector's ability to serve its citizens and enable private-sector growth. This initiative will support the public sector in undertaking the improvements and reforms necessary to achieve long-term economic success. A commitment to upholding property rights, improving the legal and regulatory framework for businesses, adopting a growth-oriented, enforceable tax structure, and developing robust capital markets will increase exports and foreign direct investment. A fair and independent judicial branch will ensure this pro-growth environment is protected and that civil society flourishes. New systems and policies will help bolster government transparency and accountability. International partners will work to eliminate the Palestinian public sector's donor dependency and put the Palestinians on a trajectory to achieve long-term fiscal sustainability. Institutions will be modernized and made more efficient to facilitate the most effective delivery of essential services for the citizens. With the support of the Palestinian leadership, this initiative can usher in a new era of prosperity and opportunity for the Palestinian people and institutionalize the policies required for successful economic transformation.

These three initiatives are more than just a vision of a promising future for the Palestinian people. They are also the foundation for an implementable plan. Capital raised through this international effort will be placed into a new fund administered by an established multilateral development bank. Accountability, transparency, anti-corruption, and conditionality safeguards will protect investments and ensure that capital is allocated efficiently and effectively. The fund's leadership will work with beneficiaries to outline annual investment guidelines, development goals, and governance reforms that will support project implementation in the areas identified within *Peace to Prosperity*. Grants, concessional loans, and other support will be distributed to projects that meet the defined criteria through a streamlined process that will enable both flexibility and accountability.

In addition to the requirement that the State of Palestine comply in all respects with the Israeli-Palestinian Peace Agreement, *Peace to Prosperity* will be conditioned upon (i) the establishment by the State of Palestine of transparent, independent, and credit-worthy financial institutions capable of engaging in international market transactions in the same manner as financial institutions of western democracies, (ii) the establishment of appropriate governance to ensure the proper use of funds, and (iii) the establishment of a legal system that protects investments and addresses commercial expectations.

The United States will work with the Palestinian Authority to identify economic projects for Al Quds and incorporate such projects into *Peace to Prosperity*.

The economic plan will empower the Palestinian people to build the society that they have aspired to establish for generations. It will allow Palestinians to realize a better future and pursue their dreams. We are confident that the international community will support this plan. Ultimately, however, the power to implement it lies in the hands of the Palestinian people.

SECTION SEVEN
SECURITY

This Vision is designed to enable Israelis and Palestinians to live in peace and to reduce the risk of terrorism.

It is unrealistic to ask the State of Israel to make security compromises that could endanger the lives of its citizens.

Appendix 2A provides a broad outline of some the acute security challenges facing the State of Israel. The goal of this Vision is to enable the parties to meet those security challenges and to enable the State of Palestine to assume as much of its security responsibilities as possible, as quickly as possible, throughout the State of Palestine.

This Vision contemplates facilitating close security coordination between the State of Israel and the State of Palestine, together with the Hashemite Kingdom of Jordan and the Arab Republic of Egypt. This section sets forth the best path to realistically achieve this goal. If the proper level of security coordination cannot be achieved, then the security of the State of Israel is nevertheless protected under this Vision.

Every country spends a very significant sum of money on its defense from external threats. The State of Palestine will not be burdened with such costs, because it will be shouldered by the State of Israel. This is a significant benefit for the economy of the State of Palestine since funds that would otherwise be spent on defense can instead be directed towards healthcare, education, infrastructure and other matters to improve Palestinians' well-being.

Upon signing the Israeli-Palestinian Peace Agreement, the State of Israel will maintain overriding security responsibility for the State of Palestine, with the aspiration that the Palestinians will be responsible for as much of their internal security as possible, subject to the provisions of this Vision. The State of Israel will work diligently to minimize its security footprint in the State of Palestine according to the principle that the more the State of Palestine does, the less the State of Israel will have to do. The State of Israel and the Hashemite Kingdom of Jordan will discuss to what extent, if any, the Hashemite

Kingdom of Jordan can assist the State of Israel and the State of Palestine in connection with security in the State of Palestine.

The criteria for Palestinian security performance (the "**SECURITY CRITERIA**") are generally outlined in <u>Appendix 2B.</u>

As the State of Palestine meets and maintains the Security Criteria, the State of Israel's involvement in security within the State of Palestine will be reduced. Both the Israelis and Palestinians have a common interest in maximizing Palestinian capability as quickly as possible. The United States and Israel will continue their work to strengthen the capabilities of the PASF.

The State of Israel will work to increase joint-cooperation with the PASF to help build its terrorism prevention capabilities. Achieving that goal in a manner that enhances the security of both countries will necessitate the following:

1. The State of Palestine shall be fully demilitarized and remain so, as outlined in <u>Appendix 2C.</u>

2. The State of Palestine will have security forces capable of maintaining internal security and preventing terror attacks within the State of Palestine and against the State of Israel, the Hashemite Kingdom of Jordan and the Arab Republic of Egypt. The mission of the State of Palestine's security forces will be public order, law enforcement, counterterrorism (working with the State of Israel, the Hashemite Kingdom of Jordan and the Arab Republic of Egypt as described below), border security (working with the State of Israel, the Hashemite Kingdom of Jordan and the Arab Republic of Egypt, as applicable, and as described below), protection of government officials and foreign dignitaries, and disaster response. These specific capabilities (i) may not (A) violate the principle that the State of Palestine in all its territory, including Gaza, shall be, and shall remain, fully demilitarized or (B) derogate the State of Israel's overriding security responsibility, and (ii) will be agreed upon by the State of Palestine and the State of Israel.

3. This security protocol is intended to continue unless and until there is a different agreement by both the State of Israel and the State of Palestine.

Over many years, the United States has supported the Palestinian Authority's efforts to counter terrorism. This partnership has established a foundation of trust that this Vision hopes to build upon. This Vision is based on the belief and expectation that the State of Palestine will continue such efforts and work towards enhancing such efforts. Once the State of Israel determines that the State of Palestine has demonstrated both a clear intention and a sustained capacity to fight terrorism, a pilot program will be initiated in an area of the West Bank portion of the State of Palestine, designated by the State of Israel, to determine if the State of Palestine is able to meet the Security Criteria. If the State of Palestine succeeds in maintaining the Security Criteria in the designated pilot area, then the pilot program will be expanded to other areas within the State of Palestine as well.

The United States will help support the State of Palestine to meet and maintain the Security Criteria. During the negotiations, the parties, in consultation with the United States, shall attempt to create acceptable initial non-binding metrics with respect to the initial pilot area which shall be acceptable to the State of Israel, and in no event less than the metrics used by either the Hashemite Kingdom of Jordan or the Arab Republic of Egypt (whichever is stricter) with respect to the Security Criteria. Because security threats evolve, the metrics are intended to be used as a guide, and will not be binding. However, the establishment of such non-binding metrics takes into account regional minimum benchmarks and allows the State of Palestine to better understand the minimum goals it is expected to achieve.

Should the State of Palestine fail to meet all or any of the Security Criteria at any time, the State of Israel will have the right to reverse the process outlined above. The State of Israel's security footprint in all or parts of the State of Palestine will then increase as a result of the State of Israel's determination of its expanded security needs and the time needed to address them.

Under the new reality of peace, the parties will enhance their bilateral security coordination in order to maintain peace, stability and a smooth implementation of the Israeli-Palestinian Peace Agreement.

As a complementary measure to the bilateral security coordination, a security review committee (the "**REVIEW COMMITTEE**") will be established that will consist of security representatives appointed by the State of Israel, the State of Palestine and the United States. The United States representative will be agreed to by the State of Israel and the State of Palestine. The Review Committee, which shall meet every 6 months, will serve as a forum to support the buildup and maintenance of the security capabilities of the State of Palestine toward meeting and maintaining the Security Criteria (see Appendix 2B), to review policy matters related to progress in implementing and maintaining the Security Criteria, and to facilitate necessary infrastructure changes and related investments (by the International Fund) on the ground.

The State of Israel, the State of Palestine, the Hashemite Kingdom of Jordan and the Arab Republic of Egypt share a common interest in preventing all forms of militant, extremist, terrorist or criminal activity from gaining a base of operations or in any way from destabilizing the State of Palestine or its neighbors. A secure, demilitarized and peaceful State of Palestine will contribute to the security needs of both parties and to regional security, as well as to economic prosperity. In furtherance of their internal security and to advance their common interests, the State of Palestine, the State of Israel, the Hashemite Kingdom of Jordan and the Arab Republic of Egypt will engage in comprehensive and enduring state-to-state cooperation.

The United States recommends the establishment of a regional security committee ("**RSC**"). The RSC's task would be to review regional counterterrorism policies and coordination. Ideally, the RSC would include security representatives from the United States, the State of Israel, the State of Palestine, the Hashemite Kingdom of Jordan, the Arab Republic of Egypt, the Kingdom of Saudi Arabia, and the United Arab Emirates.

The State of Israel will maintain at least one early-warning stations in the State of Palestine as designated on the Conceptual Map, which will be run by Israeli security forces. Uninterrupted Israeli security access to and from any early-warning station will be ensured.

To the extent reasonably possible, solely as determined by the State of Israel, the State of Israel will rely on blimps, drones and similar aerial equipment for security purposes in order to reduce the Israeli security footprint within the State of Palestine.

Although each party will be in charge of setting zoning rules and issuing building permits in their own countries, zoning and planning of the State of Palestine in the areas adjacent to the border between the State of Israel and the State of Palestine, including without limitation, the border between Jerusalem and Al Quds, will be subject to the State of Israel's overriding security responsibility.

The security plan outlined in this section results in billions of dollars in savings for international donors in lieu of creating a new multi-national security force composed of forces from the United States and/or other countries.

The parties will work together, in good faith, on security matters, to protect Israelis and Palestinians alike.

SECTION EIGHT

CROSSINGS

The threat of terrorism has reduced trust and slowed the movement of goods and people throughout the region. The goal of this vision is to have a rapid flow of goods and people through the borders in a dignified, extremely efficient system of crossings that does not compromise security.

The State of Israel will work closely with the Hashemite Kingdom of Jordan, the Arab Republic of Egypt and the State of Palestine to continue to improve the system for all border crossings. The system of border crossings will be implemented in a manner that keeps the visibility of the State of Israel's security role to a minimum. As permitted by law, security personnel at these crossings shall wear civilian uniforms with no state designation.

A board of overseers (the "**CROSSINGS BOARD**") comprised of three Israelis, three Palestinians and a United States representative shall meet quarterly to address concerns regarding the crossings. The United States representative will be agreed to by both the State of Palestine and the State of Israel. The purpose of the Crossings Board is not to interfere with the security measures at the crossings but rather to constructively find ways to improve the flow and treatment of people using the crossings. During the negotiations, the parties will develop a protocol pursuant to which people who have grievances with their treatment at the crossings that are not resolved between the parties will be addressed by the Crossings Board. The Crossings Board will develop goals and metrics by which to measure whether they are achieving its goals. Every year, the Crossings Board will provide, directly to the governments of each of the State of Palestine, the State of Israel the Hashemite Kingdom of Jordan, and the Arab Republic of Egypt, a report on performance and non-binding recommendations for improvements, along with goals for the following year.

All persons and goods will cross the borders into the State of Palestine through regulated border crossings, which will be monitored by the State of Israel. Israeli border crossing officials, using state of the art scanning and imaging technology, shall have the right to confirm that no weapons, dual-use or other security-risk related items will be allowed to enter into the State of Palestine. If an item is denied entry, the item will also be prohibited to be exported from the State of Israel into the State of Palestine in order to avoid creating a competitive advantage to Israeli businesses. To the extent any dispute related to whether or not a denial creates a competitive advantage, such dispute shall be referred to the Crossings Board. The State of Palestine will have the authority to set its own independent trade policy in order to deny import into the State of Palestine of any item for economic or legal purposes.

To combat terrorism while allowing maximum economic pursuit in the State of Palestine, all efforts will be made to mitigate the cost of production if a raw material or subcomponent of an end item is deemed dangerous and its import into the State of Palestine needs to be controlled. Rather than banning a dual use item, every effort should be made to develop transportation, storage and end-use monitoring measures to prevent the diversion of dangerous components to illicit use. Only security-vetted individuals and companies will be allowed to transport, store and utilize dual-use items and appropriate measures will be used to ensure that the dual-use raw materials or subcomponents are not used to produce weapons.

With respect to the processing of people at all crossings, during the negotiations, the parties, in consultation with the United States, shall attempt to create initial non-binding metrics acceptable to them and in no event less than the metrics used by either the Hashemite Kingdom of Jordan or the Arab Republic of Egypt (whichever is stricter). Because security threats evolve, the metrics are intended to be used as a guide, and will not be binding. However, the establishment of such non-binding metrics will allow the parties to achieve a workable, efficient and secure processing of people at all crossings, and take into account regional minimum benchmarks. Nothing in this section shall undermine the principles set forth in Appendix 2C.

GAZA CRITERIA

The people of Gaza have suffered for too long under the repressive rule of Hamas. They have been exploited as hostages and human shields, and bullied into submission. Hamas has failed the people of Gaza and has diverted money belonging to the Palestinians of Gaza, including funds provided by international donors, to attack the State of Israel, instead of using these funds to improve the lives of the people of Gaza.

Israel's withdrawal from Gaza nearly 15 years ago was meant to advance peace. Instead, Hamas, an internationally recognized terrorist group, gained control over the territory, and increased attacks on Israel, including the launching of thousands of rockets. Under the leadership of Hamas, the residents of Gaza have suffered extreme poverty and deprivation. After years of no progress the the donor community is fatigued and reluctant to make additional investments so long as the governance structure in Gaza is run by terrorists who provoke confrontations that lead to more destruction and suffering for the people of Gaza. This cycle can be broken if the international community unites to pursue a new course.

The State of Israel will implement its obligations under the Israeli-Palestinian Peace Agreement only if:

(A)

1. the Palestinian Authority or another national or international body acceptable to the State of Israel is in full control of Gaza, in a manner consistent with paragraph (B)(2) below;

2. Hamas, PIJ, and all other militias and terror organizations in Gaza are disarmed; and

3. Gaza is fully demilitarized.

During the negotiations, the parties will agree to a time frame for the compliance with items (A)(1) through (3) above.

(B)

1. if efforts to return all Israeli captives and the remains of Israeli soldiers have not have previously been successful, then upon the signing of the Israeli-Palestinian Peace Agreement, all Israeli captives and remains must be returned.

2. If Hamas is to play any role in a Palestinian government, it must commit to the path of peace with the State of Israel by adopting the Quartet principles, which include unambiguously and explicitly recognizing the State of Israel, committing to nonviolence, and accepting previous agreements and obligations between the parties, including the disarming of all terrorist groups. The United States expects that the State of Palestine's government will not include any members of Hamas, PIJ, or surrogates thereof, unless all of the foregoing shall have occurred.

The international community should be willing to provide compensation in the form of major investment for a complete and verifiable demilitarization of Gaza.

Once these criteria are met, the economic vision will be ready to be implemented in a phased approach whereby tranches of investment and state building aid will be released as milestones are achieved.

All of the criteria set forth in this section entitled "Gaza Criteria" are referred to in this Vision as the "**GAZA CRITERIA.**"

FREE TRADE ZONE

Subject to the agreement of the Hashemite Kingdom of Jordan, a free-trade zone between the Hashemite Kingdom of Jordan and the State of Palestine will be established to expedite economic cooperation between the two countries.

The location and size of the free-trade zone will be agreed upon by the parties so that the free trade zone will not interfere with current land use in the area and necessary security requirements. Goods from the free-trade zone will be exported using an airport located in the Hashemite Kingdom of Jordan.

TRADE AGREEMENT WITH THE UNITED STATES

The United States will continue to provide duty-free treatment to goods coming from all areas that enjoy such treatment today, and will negotiate a free trade agreement with the State of Palestine. The United States hopes that countries in Europe, the Middle East and elsewhere will also pursue free trade agreements with the State of Palestine.

PORT FACILITIES

Transportation is critical for economic development, regional integration and integration into the world economic market. Currently, the cost of goods born by the Palestinian people is particularly high due to transportation challenges. The lack of ports has raised the costs of Palestinian economic activity. Though the State of Palestine will include Gaza, security challenges make the building of a port in Gaza problematic for the foreseeable future. This Vision hopes to enhance Palestinian economic activity, protect Israeli security and provide a path for the State of Palestine to have its own port in Gaza in the future.

ISRAEL

The State of Israel will allow the State of Palestine to use and manage earmarked facilities at both the Haifa and Ashdod ports, without prejudice to the State of Israel's undisputed sovereignty at both of these locations. The purpose of these earmarked port facilities will be for the State of Palestine to benefit economically from access to the Mediterranean Sea, without compromising the State of Israel's security.

The role of the State of Israel at these earmarked port facilities will be limited to security functions that will ensure that all goods transported into and out of these earmarked port facilities do not pose a threat to the State of Israel. The security arrangements at these earmarked port facilities will be similar to those of other international border crossings managed by the State of Israel.

These earmarked port facilities will be used only by cargo ships. The State of Israel will help the State of Palestine establish a fast-track transportation system that will allow the State of Palestine to transport all cargo from the earmarked port facilities to the State of Palestine, subject to the State of Israel's security considerations.

The State of Palestine will be responsible for charging and collecting all taxes associated with goods entering these earmarked port facilities. All taxes collected for goods to be transported into the State of Palestine will belong to the State of Palestine.

The State of Israel and the State of Palestine will cooperate in an equitable manner with one another with respect to the traffic into and out of the ports. The parties will also assist one another in connection with joint civilian operations when needed in case of emergencies (e.g., fire, floods, etc.).

The earmarked port facilities and all ships using the earmarked port facilities shall be subject to applicable Israeli laws, including but not limited to, environmental and labor laws, and shall not be in violation of any applicable tariff agreements.

The earmarked port facilities will utilize the existing Israeli harbor, as well as existing Israeli support facilities for refueling and repairing vessels. The State of Israel and the State of Palestine shall enter into an agreement pursuant to which the State of Palestine will be able to utilize these facilities in an equitable manner. The State of Palestine will pay its equitable share of costs to maintain and repair all the shared facilities. However, there will be no rental fees payable by the State of Palestine to the State of Israel for use of, or relating to, these earmarked port facilities.

JORDAN

Subject to the consent of the Hashemite Kingdom of Jordan, the State of Palestine may use and manage an earmarked facility at the port of Aqaba, without prejudice to the Hashemite Kingdom of Jordan's undisputed sovereignty at the port of Aqaba. The purpose of the earmarked port facility will be for the State of Palestine to benefit economically from access to the Red Sea, without compromising the Hashemite Kingdom of Jordan's security.

The role of the Hashemite Kingdom of Jordan at the earmarked port facility will be limited to security functions that will ensure that all goods transported into and out of the earmarked port facility do not pose a threat to the Hashemite Kingdom of Jordan. The security arrangements at the earmarked port facility will be similar to those of other international border crossings managed by the Hashemite Kingdom of Jordan.

The earmarked port facility will be used only by cargo ships. The Hashemite Kingdom of Jordan will help the State of Palestine establish a fast-track transportation system that will allow the State of Palestine to transport all cargo from the earmarked port facility to the State of Palestine, subject to the Hashemite Kingdom of Jordan's security considerations.

The State of Palestine will be responsible for charging and collecting all taxes associated with goods entering the earmarked port facility. All taxes collected for goods to be transported into the State of Palestine will belong to the State of Palestine.

The Hashemite Kingdom of Jordan and the State of Palestine will cooperate in an equitable manner with one another with respect to the traffic into and out of the port. The parties will also assist one another in connection with joint civilian operations when needed in case of emergencies (fire, floods, etc.).

The earmarked port facility and all ships using the earmarked port facility shall be subject to applicable Jordanian laws, including but not limited to, environmental and labor laws, and shall not be in violation of any applicable tariff agreements.

The earmarked port facility will utilize the existing Jordanian harbor, as well as existing Jordanian support facilities for refueling and repairing vessels. The Hashemite Kingdom of Jordan and the State of Palestine shall enter into an agreement pursuant to which the State of Palestine will be able to utilize these facilities in an equitable manner. The State of Palestine will pay its equitable share of costs to maintain and repair all the shared facilities. The Hashemite Kingdom of Jordan shall be entitled to charge an appropriate rental fee, payable by the State of Palestine to the Hashemite Kingdom of Jordan for use of, and relating to, the earmarked port facility.

POTENTIAL GAZA PORT AND POTENTIAL AIRPORT FOR GAZA

Five years following the signing of the Israeli-Palestinian Peace Agreement and assuming the full satisfaction of the Gaza Criteria, the State of Palestine shall have the right, subject to the satisfaction of State of Israel's security and environmental requirements, to create an artificial island off the coast of Gaza to develop a port to serve Gaza (the "**GAZA PORT**"), as well as an airport for small aircraft. The specifics of this (or alternative locations for the Gaza port and small airport) will be determined during the negotiations. At such time, if any, as the Gaza Port is developed, the State of Palestine shall no longer have rights to utilize the earmarked port facilities in (i) Haifa and Ashdod, unless agreed to by the State of Israel, and (ii) Aqaba, unless agreed to by the Hashemite Kingdom of Jordan.

SECTION THIRTEEN
DEAD SEA RESORT AREA

The State of Israel will allow the State of Palestine to develop a resort area in the North of the Dead Sea without prejudice to the State of Israel's sovereignty at such location, including, without limitation, Israel's sovereignty to the shoreline. The presence of the Palestinian resort area along the coast of the Dead Sea will not alter the distribution arrangements between the Hashemite Kingdom of Jordan and the State of Israel for natural resources in the Dead Sea. The State of Israel and the State of Palestine will establish a road that will allow the Palestinians to travel from the State of Palestine to this resort area, subject to Israeli security considerations.

SECTION FOURTEEN
WATER AND WASTEWATER TREATMENT

The parties recognize mutual water rights and agree to equitably share existing cross border water sources and cooperate in making additional sources available through existing and emerging technologies. Shared aquifers will be managed for sustainable use to prevent impairing the groundwater quality or damaging the aquifers through over-extraction. Hydrological and climatic conditions, among other factors, will be considered when managing extraction. The parties will prioritize investing in desalination and other emerging technologies to produce substantial additional quantities of water for all uses and jointly seek to provide easily available, reasonably priced water to both parties. The parties agree to also focus investment in wastewater treatment and wastewater recycling and reuse to control and minimize pollution of the shared ground-waters. The parties will work together in good faith to manage the details with respect to water and wastewater treatment issues.

SECTION FIFTEEN

PRISONERS

The Israeli-Palestinian Peace Agreement will provide for the release of Palestinian prisoners and administrative detainees held in Israeli prisons, except (i) those convicted of murder or attempted murder, (ii) those convicted of conspiracy to commit murder (in each case murder includes murder by terrorism) and (iii) Israeli citizens. The release of prisoners (other than those described in clauses (i), (ii) and (iii)) will be conducted in two phases to allow for orderly transfer and resettlement. All prisoners who are released will become citizens of the State of Palestine. For the avoidance of doubt, prisoners described under clauses (i), (ii) and (iii) above shall not be released under the terms of the Israeli-Palestinian Peace Agreement.

> The first phase, to occur immediately after the signing of the Israeli-Palestinian Peace Agreement, will include minors, women, prisoners over 50 years of age, prisoners in ill health, and those who have served over two-thirds of their sentence.

> The parties will agree on the timing of the second phase, which will include the remaining eligible prisoners who have served over half their sentence.

> Any additional prisoner releases will be based on Israeli consent.

> As part of the agreement on prisoners, the State of Israel will agree to give amnesty to those Palestinians who committed offenses prior to the signing of the Israeli-Palestinian Peace Agreement, and who reside outside the State of Palestine, whose entry is approved into the State of Palestine pursuant to the Israeli-Palestinian Peace Agreement. Notwithstanding the forgoing, no amnesty will be given to any Palestinian described in clauses (i), (ii) or (iii) above, and such individuals will not be permitted entry into the State of Palestine.

> Each prisoner who is released will be required to sign a pledge to promote within their community the benefits of co-existence between Israelis and Palestinians, and to conduct themselves in a manner that models co-existence. Prisoners who refuse to sign this pledge will remain incarcerated.

> Each prisoner who is released shall have the right to seek asylum in a third country.

No Palestinian prisoners or administrative detainees will be released in accordance with this section if all Israeli captives and remains are not returned to the State of Israel.

REFUGEES

The Arab-Israeli conflict created both a Palestinian and Jewish refugee problem. Nearly the same number of Jews and Arabs were displaced by the Arab/Israeli conflict. Nearly all of the Jews have since been accepted and permanently resettled in Israel or other countries around the world. The Arabs who were displaced have, in very significant numbers, been isolated and kept from living as citizens in the many Arab countries in the region. For example, after the Kuwaiti government returned, following liberation by the United States and its coalition, it began a systematic clearing of Palestinians from the country through violence and economic pressure. The population of Palestinians in Kuwait dropped from 400,000 before the invasion to about 25,000.

The Palestinians have collectively been cruelly and cynically held in limbo to keep the conflict alive. Their Arab brothers have the moral responsibility to integrate them into their countries as the Jews were integrated into the State of Israel. Keeping the Palestinian people in limbo is a widespread issue. For example, in Lebanon, Palestinians have been discriminated against and prevented from entering the labor market for decades, even those born in Lebanon. They are for the most part barred from owning property or entering desirable occupations, including law, medicine and engineering. To gain employment, Palestinians are required to receive government issued work permits, but remarkably few are ever given to Palestinian refugees.

We must recognize that of all the Arab countries, the Kingdom of Jordan has valiantly attempted to take care of the Palestinian people in Jordan.

Proposals that demand that the State of Israel agree to take in Palestinian refugees, or that promise tens of billions of dollars in compensation for the refugees, have never been realistic and a credible funding source has never been identified. In fact, the world struggles to find sufficient funds to support the over 70 million global refugees and displaced persons. Over the decades the United States has been committed to supporting the needs of Palestinian refugees, who have suffered greatly over the last 70 years. From 1950 until and including 2017, the United States contributed approximately $6.15 billion to United Nations Relief and Works Agency (UNRWA). In the last 10 years alone, the U.S. contributed approximately $2.99 billion ($3.16 billion in 2017 terms), which accounted for 28% of all contributions to UNRWA. Unfortunately, Palestinian refugees have been treated as pawns in the broader Middle East chessboard, and empty promises have been made to them and to their host countries. A just, fair and realistic solution to the Palestinian refugee issue must be found in order to resolve the Israeli-Palestinian conflict.

The Jewish refugees who were forced to flee Arab and Muslim countries also suffered. Most settled in the State of Israel and some settled elsewhere. The Jewish refugee issue, including compensation for lost assets, must also be addressed. Additionally, the State of Israel deserves compensation for the costs of absorbing Jewish refugees from those countries. A just, fair and realistic solution for the issues relating to Jewish refugees must be implemented through an appropriate international mechanism separate from the Israel-Palestinian Peace Agreement.

This Vision contemplates that the Palestinian refugee issue will be resolved along the following lines:

GENERAL FRAMEWORK

The Israeli-Palestinian Peace Agreement shall provide for a complete end and release of any and all claims relating to refugee or immigration status. There shall be no right of return by, or absorption of, any Palestinian refugee into the State of Israel.

To be eligible for any refugee rights under the Israeli-Palestinian Peace Agreement, individuals must be in Registered Refugee status by UNRWA, as of the date of release of this Vision. The reference to the UNRWA definition of refugees is being used solely to define the universe of claimants and to provide the Trustees (as defined below) of the Palestinian Refugee Trust (as defined below) the widest flexibility to determine the appropriate distribution methodology, but should not be construed as acceptance by the United States that, in the absence of the Israeli-Palestinian Peace Agreement, refugee status should be determined by reference to this definition, including on a multi-generational, perpetual manner. UNRWA's mandate, and its multi-generational definition of who constitutes a refugee, has exacerbated the refugee crisis. Under any circumstance, individuals who have already resettled in a permanent location (to be further defined in the Israeli-Palestinian Peace Agreement) will not be eligible for resettlement, and will be eligible only for compensation as described below.

This plan envisions three options for Palestinian refugees seeking a permanent place of residence:

1. Absorption into the State of Palestine (subject to the limitations provided below);

2. Local integration in current host countries (subject to those countries consent); or

3. The acceptance of 5,000 refugees each year, for up to ten years (50,000 total refugees), in individual Organization of Islamic Cooperation member countries who agree to participate in Palestinian refugee resettlement (subject to those individual countries' agreement).

The United States will work together with other countries to establish a framework for the implementation of such options, including taking into account current host countries' concerns and limitations.

COMPENSATION AND ASSISTANCE FRAMEWORK

It is the view of the United States that while refugee compensation is important and desirable, funds will have a far greater impact on the State of Palestine's economic and social viability and on the refugees themselves if used to implement the Trump Economic Plan. The State of Palestine will be receiving substantial assistance to develop all key economic and infrastructure sectors. The Hashemite Kingdom of Jordan, which has admirably supported Palestinian refugees, will also receive benefits from the Trump Economic Plan. The Palestinian refugees already residing in the State of Palestine and those who relocate to the State of Palestine will be direct beneficiaries of this large-scale aid and investment package.

Nevertheless, we will endeavor to raise a fund to provide some compensation to Palestinian refugees. Such funds will be placed in a trust (the "**PALESTINIAN REFUGEE TRUST**") to be administered by two trustees ("**TRUSTEES**") to be appointed by the State of Palestine and the United States. The Trustees will administer the Palestinian Refugee Trust in accordance with the principles to be established by the Trustees and approved by the State of Palestine and the United States. The Trustees will work in good faith to adopt a distribution methodology to fairly compensate refugees in accordance with the priorities established by the Trustees and within the total amount of the funds collected for the Palestinian Refugee Trust.

Once the Trustees have received and analyzed refugee claims, they will allocate the funds in the Palestinian Refugee Trust to claimants in a manner that reflects those priorities.

It must be stressed that many Palestinian refugees in the Middle East come from war torn countries, such as Syria and Lebanon that are extremely hostile toward the State of Israel. To address this concern, a committee of Israelis and Palestinians will be formed to address this issue and to resolve outstanding disputes over the entry in the State of Palestine of Palestinian refugees from any location. The rights of Palestinian refugees to immigrate to the State of Palestine shall be limited in accordance with agreed security arrangements.

Furthermore, the rate of movement of refugees from outside Gaza and the West Bank into the State of Palestine shall be agreed to by the parties and regulated by various factors, including economic forces and incentive structures, such that the rate of entry does not outpace or overwhelm the development of infrastructure and the economy of the State of Palestine, or increase security risks to the State of Israel. This rate of movement should be adjusted, as appropriate, with the passage of time.

Upon the signing of the Israeli-Palestinian Peace Agreement, Palestinian refugee status will cease to exist, and UNWRA will be terminated and its responsibilities transitioned to the relevant governments. Part of the Trump Economic Plan will go toward the replacement of refugee camps in the State of Palestine with new housing developments in the State of Palestine. Thus, the Israeli-Palestinian Peace Agreement will lead to the dismantling of all Palestinian refugee camps and the building of permanent housing.

FOUNDATIONS OF A PALESTINIAN STATE

The transition to statehood is complex and fraught with peril. The region cannot absorb another failed state, another state not committed to human rights or the rule of law. A Palestinian State, just like any other state, must combat all forms of terrorism and be accountable to its neighbors to be a productive and non-threatening member of the international community. For the sake of its future citizens and neighbors, it is critical that the State of Palestine have the necessary foundational elements to give it a high probability of succeeding.

The following criteria are a predicate to the formation of a Palestinian State and must be determined to have occurred by the State of Israel and the United States, jointly, acting in good faith, after consultation with the Palestinian Authority:

> The Palestinians shall have implemented a governing system with a constitution or another system for establishing the rule of law that provides for freedom of press, free and fair elections, respect for human rights for its citizens, protections for religious freedom and for religious minorities to observe their faith, uniform and fair enforcement of law and contractual rights, due process under law, and an independent judiciary with appropriate legal consequences and punishment established for violations of the law.

> The Palestinians shall have established transparent, independent, and credit-worthy financial institutions capable of engaging in international market transactions in the same manner as financial institutions of western democracies with appropriate governance to prevent corruption and ensure the proper use of such funds, and a legal system to protect investments and to address market-based commercial expectations. The State of Palestine should meet the independent objective criteria to join the International Monetary Fund.

> The Palestinians shall have ended all programs, including school curricula and textbooks, that serve to incite or promote hatred or antagonism towards its neighbors, or which compensate or incentivize criminal or violent activity.

> The Palestinians shall have achieved civilian and law enforcement control over all of its territory and demilitarized its population.

> The Palestinians shall have complied with all the other terms and conditions of this Vision.

The United States, the State of Israel and all regional neighbors will work productively and in good faith with the Palestinian leadership to provide the necessary assistance to the achievement of the criteria listed above.

As it transitions to an era of state governance, the Palestinian leadership will benefit from international assistance in crafting the political and logistical instrumentalities of statehood.

The international community should mobilize a worldwide effort to assist the Palestinians to achieve proper governance. By virtue of territorial proximity, cultural affinity and family ties, the Hashemite Kingdom of Jordan is well placed to play a distinctive role in providing this assistance in fields such as law, medicine, education, municipal services, historic preservation and institution building. In a manner consistent with the dignity and autonomy of a future State of Palestine, the Hashemite Kingdom of Jordan will offer long-term, on-the-ground assistance in designing relevant institutions and procedures and training of relevant personnel. The objective of such assistance will be to help the Palestinians build strong and well governed institutions.

Other countries will be encouraged to provide assistance to the Palestinians in areas in which they have special experience or expertise. The international community recognizes that the implementation of this Vision will necessitate the expansion of the Palestinian government's reach and capacity to provide services to additional people across a larger area. The international community will provide technical assistance across the spectrum of services that the Palestinian government will need to provide, including security. Donors will place particular emphasis on upgrading infrastructure, equipment, and mobility and communication capacity to ensure the Palestinian government can professionally police a future State of Palestine.

Once these measures are completed the United States will encourage other countries to welcome the State of Palestine as a full member in international organizations. However, the State of Palestine may not join any international organization if such membership would contradict commitments of the State of Palestine to demilitarization and cessation of political and judicial warfare against the State of Israel. Through such membership in international organizations, other countries will encourage the participation of the State of Palestine as a respected and responsible member of the international community.

The State of Palestine will be able to establish diplomatic relations with other countries.

EDUCATION AND CULTURE OF PEACE

As President Trump has said: "Peace can never take root in an environment where violence is tolerated, funded and even rewarded." Therefore, it is very important that education focuses on peace to ensure that future generations are committed to peace and to ensure that the Israeli-Palestinian Peace Agreement can endure. Promoting a culture of peace will be an important element of the Israeli-Palestinian Peace Agreement with the goal of creating an environment that embraces the values of coexistence and mutual respect throughout the region.

The creation of a culture of peace should include an end to incitement, including in government-controlled media, as well as an end to the glorification of violence, terrorism and martyrdom. It should also prohibit hostile propaganda, as well as textbooks, curriculum and related materials contrary to the goal of the Israeli-Palestinian Peace Agreement, including the denial of one another's right to exist.

A joint Commission on Acceptance and Tolerance will be created to focus on steps that can be taken help the people from both countries heal the wounds that have been created by this conflict and bring the people closer together through dialogue.

ISRAELI–ARAB RELATIONSHIPS;
REGIONAL ECONOMIC PARTNERSHIPS

The decisions of the Arab Republic of Egypt and the Hashemite Kingdom of Jordan to sign peace treaties with the State of Israel were major historic breakthroughs. Nevertheless, significant and broader cooperation between these countries should be developed for the benefit of the Arab Republic of Egypt, the Hashemite Kingdom of Jordan, and the State of Israel. The involvement of the Kingdom of Saudi Arabia in the Arab Peace Initiative increased the number of potential peace partners and introduced important concepts into the peace process. Much appreciation is owed to the Kingdom of Saudi Arabia for its role in the creation of the Arab Peace Initiative, which inspired some of the ideas contemplated by this Vision.

The goal of this Vision is to have the Arab states fully cooperate with the State of Israel for the benefit of all the countries in the region. For example, there should be flights between Arab countries and Israel to promote cross-tourism, and to better enable Arabs to visit Muslim and Christian holy sites in Israel.

The United States will strongly encourage Arab countries to begin to normalize their relations with the State of Israel and negotiate lasting peace agreements.

Economic ties between the State of Israel and its neighbors should be expanded in the interests of all sides, particularly given the interests of the Arab countries to move away from economies based on fossil fuels to economies based on new infrastructure and technology. By integrating their transportation infrastructure, the countries in the region can become a global hub for the movement of goods and services from Asia to Africa and Europe. Such integration between the State of Israel, the State of Palestine and the Hashemite Kingdom of Jordan will allow all three countries to work together to help move goods from Europe to the Persian Gulf and vice versa. The State of Israel and the Arab countries, including the State of Palestine, should establish strong economic partnerships and trade agreements. There should be a particular focus on significantly improving the economic and tourism sectors of the State of Palestine, the Hashemite Kingdom of Jordan and the Arab Republic of Egypt.

The emergence of this new reality of regional integration will require a fundamental change in international politics. In the diplomatic sphere, in particular, the Arab countries, along with the State of Palestine, should cease to support anti-Israel initiatives at the United Nations and in other multilateral bodies. In particular, they should not lend their support to any efforts intended to delegitimize the State of Israel. These countries are expected to end any boycott of the State of Israel and oppose the Boycott, Divestment, and Sanctions (commonly referred to as BDS) movement and any other effort to boycott the State of Israel. The United States views the BDS movement as destructive towards peace, and will oppose any activity that advances BDS or other restrictive trade practices targeting Israel.

Revisionist initiatives that question the Jewish people's authentic roots in the State of Israel should also cease. Those initiatives fly in the face of not only Jewish and Christian history, but Islamic history as well. An important goal of this Vision is for the State of Israel to be treated by all as a legitimate part of the international community.

NEW OPPORTUNITIES FOR REGIONAL SECURITY INITIATIVES

In confronting common threats and in pursuing common interests, previously unimaginable opportunities and alliances are emerging.

The State of Israel, the State of Palestine and the Arab countries will work together to counter Hezbollah, ISIS, Hamas (if Hamas does not reorient in accordance with the Gaza Criteria), and all other terrorist groups and organizations, as well as other extremist groups.

The threats posed by Iran's radical regime has led to a new reality where the State of Israel and its Arab neighbors now share increasingly similar perceptions of the threats to their security. Furthermore, Israel and its Arab neighbors increasingly share a vision of stability and economic prosperity for the region. Enhanced strategic cooperation between countries in the region would set the stage for diplomatic breakthroughs and a broader regional security architecture in the future.

The State of Israel is not a threat to the region whatsoever. Economic conditions and Iran's malign activities, however, pose an existential threat to many of the region's states. Integrating Israel into the region will allow it to assist across a wide range of economic challenges as well as counter the threats of Iran. The Iranian attack on Aramco facilities in Saudi Arabia in 2019, for example, shocked the world's economy and makes clear the necessity for the countries of the region to work together on security.

The State of Israel and the Arab countries have already discovered their common interests in combating terrorist groups and organizations and the common danger posed by an expansionist Iran. These countries also face similar security challenges in the Mediterranean and the Red Sea. They should work together, along with the United States, to protect the freedom of navigation through international straits that are increasingly subject to the threat of Iran, its proxy forces, and terrorist groups.

These shared interest in the region should be expressed in closer ties between the State of Israel and the Gulf Cooperation Council. Moreover, the State of Palestine, the Arab Republic of Egypt, the Hashemite Kingdom of Jordan and the State of Israel (and such additional countries in the region who wish to join) should form an Organization for Security and Cooperation in the Middle East (the "**OSCME**"), similar to the model used by the Organization for Security and Co-operation in Europe. The OSCME mandate should include, among others, issues such as early warning of conflicts, conflict prevention, and crisis management.

SECTION TWENTY
MUTUAL RECOGNITION BETWEEN NATION STATES

The Israeli-Palestinian Peace Agreement will provide that the parties recognize the State of Palestine as the nation state of the Palestinian people and the State of Israel as the nation state of the Jewish people.

END OF CLAIMS / END OF CONFLICT

The Israeli-Palestinian Peace Agreement will end the conflict between Israelis and Palestinians, and end all claims between the parties. The foregoing will be proposed in (i) a new UN Security Council resolution, and (ii) a new UN General Assembly resolution.

CONDUCT DURING NEGOTIATIONS

We hope that the parties will seize the opportunity, embrace this vision and begin negotiations. During the negotiations the parties should conduct themselves in a manner that comports with this Vision, and in a way that prepares their respective peoples for peace.

During the peace negotiations, the parties are expected to do the following:

THE STATE OF ISRAEL

In areas of the West Bank that are not contemplated by this Vision to be part of the State of Israel, Israel will not:

1. Build any new settlement towns, expand existing settlements or advance plans to build in those areas;

2. Expand any of the Israeli enclaves referred to in Section 4 or advance plans to expand those enclaves in those areas beyond their current footprint;

3. Demolish any structure existing as of the date of this Vision and secure the necessary legislative and/or legal decisions to ensure such an outcome. This moratorium does not preclude demolition of any illegal construction, where such construction was initiated following the release of this Vision. This moratorium does not apply to the demolition of any structure that poses a safety risk, as determined by the State of Israel, or punitive demolitions following acts of terrorism.

In Palestinian enclaves referred to in Section 4, the legal status quo will prevail and the State of Israel will enable the development of those Palestinian communities within their current footprint.

PALESTINIANS

The PLO and the Palestinian Authority shall:

1. Refrain from any attempt to join any international organization without the consent of the State of Israel;

2. Take no action, and shall dismiss all pending actions, against the State of Israel, the United States and any of their citizens before the International Criminal Court, the International Court of Justice, and all other tribunals;

3. Take no action against any Israeli or United States citizen before Interpol or any non-Israeli or United States (as applicable) legal system;

4. Take all necessary actions to immediately terminate the paying of salaries to terrorists serving sentences in Israeli prisons, as well as to the families of deceased terrorists (collectively, the "**PRISONER & MARTYR PAYMENTS**") and to develop humanitarian and welfare programs to provide essential services and support to Palestinians in need that are not based upon the commission of terrorist acts. The goal is to change the applicable laws, in a manner that is consistent with the laws of the United States, and completely cease making Prisoner and Martyr Payments by the time of signing of the Israeli-Palestinian Peace Agreement; and

5. Further the development of institutions necessary for self-governance.

THE UNITED STATES

To the extent permitted by law, the United States shall:

A. Allow the Office of the General Delegation of the Palestine Liberation Organization to reopen;

B. Open a liasion mission to the Palestinian Authority at an appropriate location within the territory designated for the State of Palestine, as determined by the United States;

C. Take appropriate steps to resume U.S. assistance to the West Bank and Gaza, to the extent reasonable and appropriate, in consultation with the U.S. Congress; and

D. Work with the international community to support new initiatives for the Palestinian people including, programs to improve the delivery of electricity and water, ease the movement of goods and help create jobs.

APPENDIX 1

CONCEPTUAL MAPS

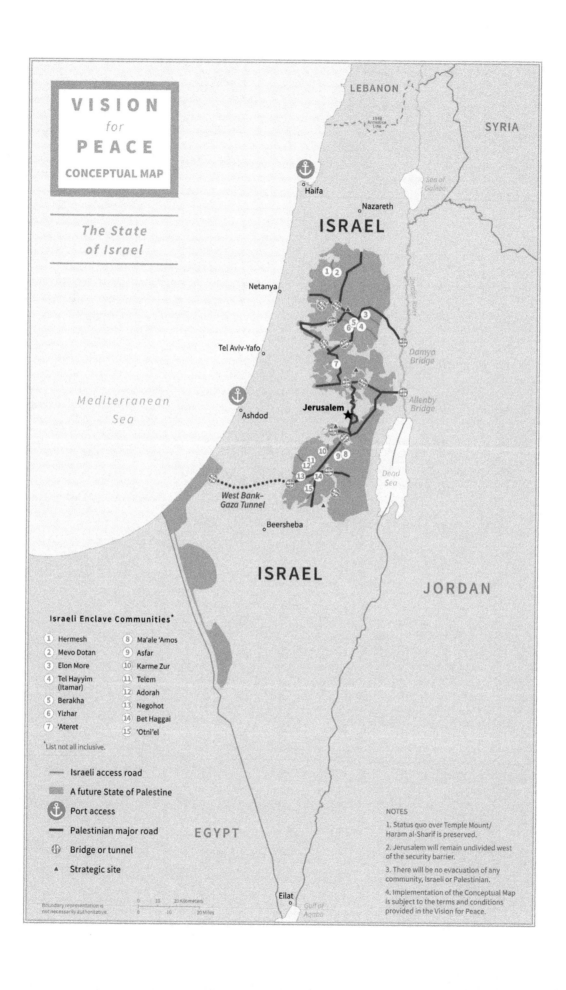

VISION for PEACE

CONCEPTUAL MAP

The State of Israel

LEBANON

SYRIA

1949 Armistice Line

Sea of Galilee

Haifa

Nazareth

ISRAEL

Netanya

① ②

③

⑤
⑥ ④

Tel Aviv-Yafo

Damya Bridge

⑦

Jerusalem

Allenby Bridge

Mediterranean Sea

Ashdod

⑩
⑨ ⑧
⑪
⑫
⑬ ⑭
⑮

Dead Sea

West Bank–Gaza Tunnel

Beersheba

ISRAEL

JORDAN

Israeli Enclave Communities*

① Hermesh	⑧ Ma'ale 'Amos
② Mevo Dotan	⑨ Asfar
③ Elon More	⑩ Karme Zur
④ Tel Hayyim (Itamar)	⑪ Telem
	⑫ Adorah
⑤ Berakha	⑬ Negohot
⑥ Yizhar	⑭ Bet Haggai
⑦ 'Ateret	⑮ 'Otni'el

*List not all inclusive.

— Israeli access road

░ A future State of Palestine

⚓ Port access

— Palestinian major road

⊕ Bridge or tunnel

▲ Strategic site

EGYPT

Eilat

Gulf of Aqaba

Boundary representation is not necessarily authoritative.

0   10   20 Kilometers
0   10   20 Miles

NOTES

1. Status quo over Temple Mount/ Haram al-Sharif is preserved.

2. Jerusalem will remain undivided west of the security barrier.

3. There will be no evacuation of any community, Israeli or Palestinian.

4. Implementation of the Conceptual Map is subject to the terms and conditions provided in the Vision for Peace.

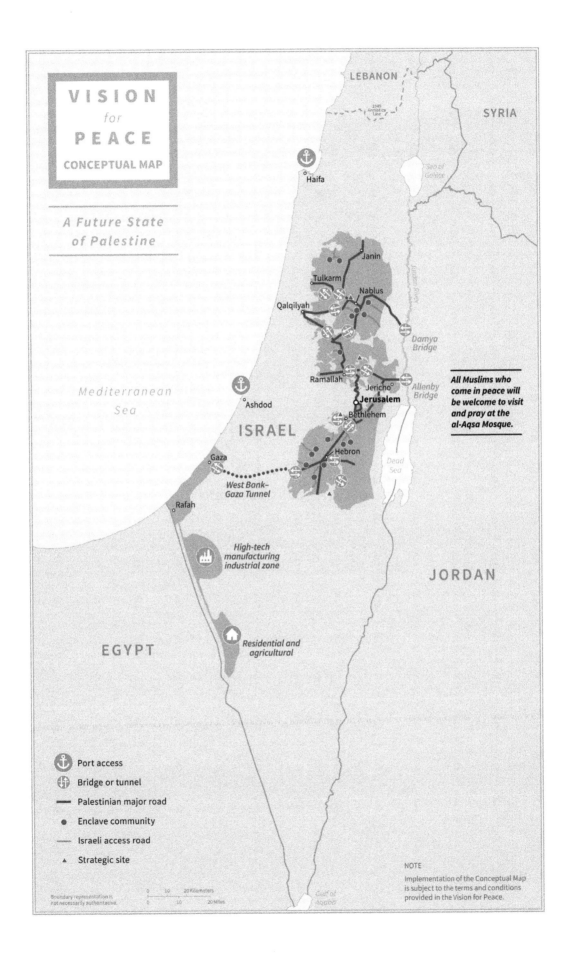

VISION
for
PEACE
CONCEPTUAL MAP

*A Future State
of Palestine*

LEBANON

SYRIA

1949 Armistice Line

Sea of Galilee

Haifa

Mediterranean
Sea

Janin

Tulkarm

Nablus

Qalqilyah

Jordan River

Damya
Bridge

Ramallah

Jericho

**All Muslims who
come in peace will
be welcome to visit
and pray at the
al-Aqsa Mosque.**

Ashdod

Jerusalem

Allenby
Bridge

ISRAEL

Bethlehem

Dead
Sea

Gaza

Hebron

West Bank–
Gaza Tunnel

Rafah

*High-tech
manufacturing
industrial zone*

JORDAN

EGYPT

*Residential and
agricultural*

Port access

Bridge or tunnel

Palestinian major road

Enclave community

Israeli access road

Strategic site

Boundary representation is
not necessarily authoritative.

0   10   20 Kilometers
0   10   20 Miles

NOTE

Implementation of the Conceptual Map
is subject to the terms and conditions
provided in the Vision for Peace.

Gulf of
Aqaba

APPENDIX 2A

SECURITY CONSIDERATIONS

Since the moment of its establishment, the State of Israel has not known a single day of peace with all of its neighbors. It has fought numerous defensive wars, some existential in nature, as well as asymmetric battles with terrorist groups. The State of Israel remains in a state of war with two of its neighbors (Lebanon and Syria) and is exposed to extraordinary risk from the rocket and missile arsenals on its northern border. The State of Israel has repeatedly confronted indiscriminate rocket fire from the Gaza Strip, and the State of Israel faces a grave threat from Iranian ballistic missiles, including missiles capable of carrying nuclear warheads, and belligerent public threats from Iran to wipe the State of Israel off the map.

Since the Six-Day War in 1967, the West Bank and Gaza have figured prominently in the State of Israel's security, largely because of geo-strategic considerations. Looking at the West Bank alone, the area is adjacent to the State of Israel's coastal plain, where 70% of the State of Israel's population is concentrated along with roughly 80% of its industrial capacity.

Prior to 1967, Israel's coastal plain was only 9 miles wide at its narrowest point. While the Israeli coastal plain is at sea level, the West Bank contains a north-south hill ridge providing any hostile force the ability to topographically dominate the most sensitive parts of Israel's national infrastructure. This includes, for example, Ben Gurion Airport, Israel's high tech industries, and its north-south road networks that connect Tel Aviv to Haifa in the north and Jerusalem in the east.

The security portion of this Vision was developed based on our best understanding of the security requirements of the State of Israel, as presented by successive Israeli governments to the United States.

THE STATE OF ISRAEL'S SECURITY NEEDS

THE JORDAN VALLEY

The Jordan River lies approximately 1,300 feet below sea level, but it is situated right next to a north-south hill ridge that reaches approximately 3,318 feet at its highest point. That means that the Jordan Valley provides a steep, approximately 4,600 foot physical barrier against an external attack from the east. Israeli forces deployed along the eastern slopes of the West Bank hill ridge could hold off a numerically superior army until the State of Israel completed its reserve mobilization, which could take 48 hours. The State of Israel does not currently have a security concern with the Hashemite Kingdom of Jordan, with which it has had a peace treaty since 1994, but rather with other Middle Eastern powers that might seek to forcibly use Jordanian territory as a platform of attack against the State of Israel.

The Jordan Valley is not only significant with regard to conventional attacks against the State of Israel, but also with regard to terrorism. Following its unilateral withdrawal from the Gaza Strip, the State of Israel learned the implications of losing control of the external perimeter of contested territory for counterinsurgency warfare. Gaza became a safe haven, not only for Hamas, but also for international Jihadi groups like the PIJ that undermined the security of Egypt in the Sinai. If such groups infiltrated the West Bank, they could create a chaotic security situation for the Hashemite Kingdom of Jordan, as well as for the State of Israel.

If the State of Israel withdrew from the Jordan Valley, it would have significant implications for regional security in the Middle East.

SECURE LINES OF SUPPLY TO THE JORDAN VALLEY

The State of Israel must assure for itself secure lines of supply for its forces in the Jordan Valley and the ability to move its military personnel and material into and out of the region.

BEN GURION AIRPORT PERIMETER

Israel's main international airport, Ben Gurion Airport, is 5.9 miles away from the pre-1967 line. Among the threats to airport security today are shoulder-fired anti-aircraft missiles used by terrorist organizations. Known as Man-Portable Air Defense Systems or MANPADS, these systems are proliferating across the Middle East.

Special security standards for airport defense are necessary to prevent threats to Ben Gurion Airport and nearby air traffic.

ISRAELI CONTROL OF THE AIRSPACE WEST OF THE JORDAN RIVER

Because of its narrow size, the State of Israel lacks the time and the space many other countries enjoy to address fast approaching threats, especially airborne threats. The distance from the Jordan River to the Mediterranean is approximately 40 miles. A modern combat aircraft can cover that distance in under three minutes. For the Israeli Air Force to scramble fighters takes approximately three minutes. If the State of Israel did not maintain control of the West Bank's airspace, it would not have adequate time to defend against incoming hostile aircraft or missiles. For that reason, in any peace arrangement, the State of Israel must have operational control over the airspace west of the Jordan River.

THE PROBLEM WITH INTERNATIONAL FORCES

The State of Israel has experienced the failure of international troops in Sinai (before 1967), Lebanon, Gaza, and the Golan. Given its experience, Israel's first doctrine of security – that it must be able to defend itself by itself – is as salient as ever. It is a critical strategic interest of the United States that the State of Israel remain strong and secure, protected by the IDF, and continue to remain an anchor of stability in the region.

IRAN

In the last few years, Iran has become an influential factor in areas of the Middle East, which could impinge upon Israeli security. Iran's strategy seeks to encircle Israel, using Lebanon, Syria and Gaza, and encircle the Kingdom of Saudi Arabia Iraq, Bahrain and Yemen. Iran hopes to establish a "land bridge" that stretches from the Iran-Iraq border to the Mediterranean Sea. All of Iran's activity must be taken into account in determining the State of Israel's security needs.

APPENDIX 2B

SECURITY CRITERIA

Specific Security Criteria shall include the following:

1. The State of Palestine's counterterrorism system must encompass all elements of counterterrorism, from initial detection of illicit activity to longtime incarceration of perpetrators. Included in the system must be: intelligence officers to detect potential terrorist activity, specially trained counterterrorism forces to raid sites and arrest perpetrators, forensics experts to conduct site exploitation, pretrial detention officers to ensure the retention of prisoners, prosecutors and judges to issue warrants and conduct trials, and post-trial detention officers to ensure prisoners serve their sentences. The system should include stand-alone detention facilities and vetted personnel.

2. The State of Palestine will erect and maintain a legal system that clearly confronts terrorism, including by:

   a. Establishing and enforcing laws banning all terror activity and terror organizations and prohibiting all incitement to terrorism, as well as the financing of such activity and organizations;

   b. Effectively prosecuting and appropriately sentencing those involved, both directly or indirectly, in terror activity;

   c. Ending all payments rewarding terrorism, directly or indirectly, to those involved in terror activity or their families.

3. The breadth and depth of the anti-terror activities of the State of Palestine will be determined by:

   a. The extent of arrests and interdictions of suspects, perpetrators and accomplices;

   b. The systematic and comprehensive nature of investigations and interrogations to root out all terror networks and infrastructure;
   c. Indictments and the extent of punishments;

   d. The systematic and comprehensive nature of interdiction efforts to seize weapons and explosives and prevent the manufacturing of weapons and explosives;

   e. The success of efforts to prevent infiltration of terrorists and terror organizations into the security forces of the State of Palestine;

4. During the negotiations the parties, in consultation with the United States, shall attempt to create acceptable initial non-binding metrics with respect to the Security Criteria that are acceptable to the State of Israel, and in no event less stringent than the metrics used by either the Hashemite Kingdom of Jordan or the Arab Republic of Egypt (whichever is stricter) with respect to the Security Criteria. Because security threats evolve, the metrics are intended to be used as a guide, and will not be binding. However, the establishment of such non-binding metrics will allow the State of Palestine to better understand the minimum goals they are expected to achieve, and take into account regional minimum benchmarks.

APPENDIX 2C

DEMILITARIZATION CRITERIA AND OTHER SECURITY ARRANGEMENTS

In addition to the overriding security responsibility over the State of Palestine, the State of Israel will be responsible for security at all international crossings into the State of Palestine. With respect to the Rafah crossing, specific arrangements will be agreed upon between the Arab Republic of Egypt and the State of Israel to accomplish the security needs contemplated by this Vision.

The State of Israel will continue to maintain control over the airspace and the electromagnetic spectrum west of the Jordan river. During the negotiation period, the parties should negotiate in good faith relevant financial issues.

The Israeli Navy will have the right to block prohibited weapons and weapon-making materials from entering the State of Palestine, including Gaza.

The State of Palestine will not have the right to forge military, intelligence or security agreements with any state or organization that adversely affect the State of Israel's security, as determined by the State of Israel. The State of Palestine will not be able to develop military or paramilitary capabilities inside or outside of the State of Palestine.

A demilitarized State of Palestine will be prohibited from possessing capabilities that can threaten the State of Israel including: weapons systems such as combat aircraft (manned and unmanned); heavy armored vehicles; mines; missiles; rockets; heavy machine guns; laser/radiating weapons; anti-air; anti-armor; anti-ship; military intelligence; offensive cyber and electronic warfare capabilities; production facilities and procurement mechanisms for weapons systems; military infrastructure and training facilities; or any weapons of mass destruction.

Any expansion of Palestinian security capabilities beyond the capabilities existing on the date this Vision is released shall be subject to agreement with the State of Israel.

The State of Israel will maintain the right to dismantle and destroy any facility in the State of Palestine that is used for the production of prohibited weapons or for other hostile purposes. While the State of Israel will use its best efforts to minimize incursions into the State of Palestine, the State of Israel will retain the right to engage in necessary security measures to ensure that the State of Palestine remains demilitarized and non-threatening to the State of Israel, including from terrorist threats.

PART B
ECONOMIC FRAMEWORK

CONTENTS

FOREWORD

Generations of Palestinians have lived without knowing peace, and the West Bank and Gaza have fallen into a protracted crisis. Yet the Palestinian story will not end here. The Palestinian people continue their historic endeavor to build a better future for their children.

Peace to Prosperity is a vision to empower the Palestinian people to build a prosperous and vibrant Palestinian society. It consists of three initiatives that will support distinct pillars of the Palestinian society: the economy, the people, and the government. With the potential to facilitate more than $50 billion in new investment over ten years, *Peace to Prosperity* represents the most ambitious and comprehensive international effort for the Palestinian people to date. It has the ability to fundamentally transform the West Bank and Gaza and to open a new chapter in Palestinian history—one defined, not by adversity and loss, but by freedom and dignity.

The first initiative will **UNLEASH THE ECONOMIC POTENTIAL** of the Palestinians. By developing property and contract rights, the rule of law, anti-corruption measures, capital markets, a pro-growth tax structure, and a low-tariff scheme with reduced trade barriers, this initiative envisions policy reforms coupled with strategic infrastructure investments that will improve the business environment and stimulate private-sector growth. Hospitals, schools, homes, and businesses will secure reliable access to affordable electricity, clean water, and digital services. Billions of dollars of new investment will flow into various sectors of the Palestinian economy; businesses will have access to capital; and the markets of the West Bank and Gaza will be connected with key trading partners, including Egypt, Israel, Jordan, and Lebanon. The resulting economic growth has the potential to end the current unemployment crisis and transform the West Bank and Gaza into a center of opportunity.

The second initiative will **EMPOWER THE PALESTINIAN PEOPLE** to realize their ambitions. Through new data-driven, outcomes-based education options at home, expanded online education platforms, increased vocational and technical training, and the prospect of international exchanges, this initiative will enhance and expand a variety of programs that directly improve the well-being of the Palestinian people. It will strengthen the Palestinian educational system and ensure that students can fulfill their academic goals and be prepared for the workforce. Equally important, access to quality healthcare will be dramatically improved, as Palestinian hospitals and clinics will be outfitted with the latest healthcare technology and equipment. In addition, new opportunities for cultural and recreational activities will improve the quality of life of the Palestinian people. From parks and cultural institutions, to athletic facilities and libraries, this initiative's projects will enrich public life throughout the West Bank and Gaza.

The third initiative will **ENHANCE PALESTINIAN GOVERNANCE**, improving the public sector's ability to serve its citizens and enable private-sector growth. This initiative will support the public sector in undertaking the improvements and reforms necessary to achieve long-term economic success. A commitment to upholding property rights, improving the legal and regulatory framework for businesses, adopting a growth-oriented, enforceable tax structure, and developing robust capital markets will increase exports and foreign direct investment. A fair and independent judicial branch will ensure this pro-growth environment is protected and that civil society flourishes. New systems and policies will help bolster government transparency and accountability. International partners will work to eliminate the Palestinian public sector's donor dependency and put the Palestinians on a trajectory to achieve long-term fiscal sustainability. Institutions will be modernized and made more efficient to facilitate the most effective delivery of essential services for the citizens. With the support of the Palestinian leadership, this initiative can usher in a new era of freedom and opportunity for the Palestinian people and institutionalize the policies required for successful economic transformation.

These three initiatives are more than just a vision of a promising future for the Palestinian people—they are also the foundation for an implementable plan. Capital raised through this international effort will be placed into a new fund administered by an established multilateral development bank. Accountability, transparency, anti-corruption, and conditionality safeguards will protect investments and ensure that capital is allocated efficiently and effectively. The fund's leadership will work with beneficiary countries to outline annual investment guidelines, development goals, and governance reforms that will support project implementation in the areas identified within *Peace to Prosperity*. Grants, concessional loans, and other support will be distributed to projects that meet the defined criteria through a streamlined process that will enable both flexibility and accountability.

If implemented, *Peace to Prosperity* will empower the Palestinian people to build the society that they have aspired to establish for generations. This vision will allow the Palestinians to see a better future and realize an opportunity to pursue their dreams. With the support of the international community, this vision is within reach. Ultimately, however, the power to unlock it lies in the hands of the Palestinian people. Only through peace can the Palestinians achieve prosperity.

PEACE TO PROSPERITY: OVERALL VISION GOALS
WITHIN 10 YEARS

MORE THAN DOUBLE PALESTINIAN
GROSS DOMESTIC PRODUCT

1 MILLION

CREATE OVER ONE MILLION PALESTINIAN JOBS

REDUCE THE PALESTINIAN UNEMPLOYMENT
RATE TO NEARLY SINGLE DIGITS

REDUCE THE PALESTINIAN
POVERTY RATE BY 50 PERCENT

## CHAPTER ONE

UNLEASHING ECONOMIC POTENTIAL

*A lasting peace agreement will ensure a future of
economic opportunity for all Palestinians.*

The first initiative of *Peace to Prosperity* will establish a new foundation for the Palestinian economy, generating rapid economic growth and job creation. This part of the plan is built around four core programs and will be supported by an institutional foundation for economic growth and business investment. *Peace to Prosperity* will create a business environment that provides investors with confidence that their assets will be secure by improving property rights, the rule of law, fiscal sustainability, capital markets, and anti-corruption policies.

The first program will reduce constraints on Palestinian economic growth by **OPENING THE WEST BANK AND GAZA** to regional and global markets. Major investments in transportation and infrastructure will help the West Bank and Gaza integrate with neighboring economies, increasing the competitiveness of Palestinian exports and reducing the complications of transport and travel. To complement these investments, this program will also support steps to improve Palestinian cooperation with Egypt, Israel, and Jordan, with the goal of reducing regulatory barriers to the movement of Palestinian goods and people.

The second program will support the Palestinian economy by **CONSTRUCTING ESSENTIAL INFRASTRUCTURE** that the Palestinian people and their businesses need to flourish. This program will facilitate billions of dollars of investment in the electricity, water, and telecommunications sectors, increasing generation capacity while creating efficient transmission and distribution networks. The applicable authorities will receive training and assistance to manage this infrastructure and to increase competition to keep costs low for consumers.

The third program focuses on **PROMOTING PRIVATE-SECTOR GROWTH** with the potential to reduce unemployment to nearly single digits and to create over a million new Palestinian jobs. Following the adoption of key policy reforms and the construction of essential infrastructure, *Peace to Prosperity* envisions extraordinary private-sector investment in entrepreneurship, small businesses, tourism, agriculture, housing, manufacturing, and natural resources. The goal of early-stage investment will be to remove constraints to growth and to target key projects that build momentum, generate jobs, and increase gross domestic product (GDP). From the father working in his shop to support his family, to the young college graduate building her first company, Palestinians working throughout the private sector will benefit from this program.

The fourth program encourages **STRENGTHENING REGIONAL DEVELOPMENT AND INTEGRATION**, creates new opportunities for Palestinian businesses, and increases commerce with neighboring countries. This program will boost the economies of Egypt, Israel, Jordan, and Lebanon and reduce trade barriers across the region. Increased cooperation between trading partners will support companies in these countries, which are seeking to develop international business, particularly in the West Bank and Gaza. This program will help the Palestinian private sector capitalize on growth opportunities by improving access to strong, neighboring economies.

UNLEASHING ECONOMIC POTENTIAL:

GOALS

> Increase Palestinian exports as a percentage of GDP from 17 to 40

> Ensure continual availability of affordable electricity in the West Bank and Gaza

> Double the potable water supply per capita available to the Palestinians

> Enable Palestinian high-speed data services

> Increase the foreign direct investment share of Palestinian GDP from 1.4 percent to 8 percent

UNLEASHING ECONOMIC POTENTIAL BY BUILDING
A FOUNDATION FOR GROWTH AND BUSINESS INVESTMENT

STRATEGY FOR REFORM

Successful economic transformations draw from core principles to build critical institutions and implement policy reforms that attract business investment and sustain long-term, private-sector-driven growth. Thriving business-friendly countries like **South Korea, Singapore, Taiwan, and Japan** built modern economies with an emphasis on investment-led growth, robust infrastructure development, and strong exports. In addition, property rights, the rule of law, fiscal responsibility and independence, capital markets, and anti-corruption safeguards are crucial elements in this vision's strategy for growth. Peace to Prosperity embraces these fundamental principles and prioritizes their role in the Palestinian people's journey toward sustained economic success. Advancing these core policy and regulatory reforms, along with supporting businesses and providing technical assistance, will create the business environment needed to foster an economic transformation capable of benefiting the generations to come.

❯ BREAKOUT VENTURE

PROJECT:
Startup Equity-Matching and
Lending Facilities

LOCATION:
West Bank and Gaza

FINANCING:
$100 million in grant equity funding
$300 million in concessional financing

PROJECT OVERVIEW:
This project will support the creation of equity-matching and lending facilities focused on Palestinian startups and emerging technology companies. The equity-matching component will encourage venture capital and private equity firms to invest in Palestinian startups. The lending component will incentivize Palestinian banks to increase their lending to qualified startups. Together, these facilities will help Palestinian entrepreneurs attract the equity and debt capital they need to build the next generation of innovative Palestinian companies.

HUMAN CAPITAL

Creating the foundation for growth and business investment begins with the Palestinian people. Palestinians, like all people, dream of a better future for themselves and future generations and aspire to professional success. *Peace to Prosperity* offers a path to realize those dreams. Drawing from models used by **Germany and Sweden**, this program lays out a strategy for training, developing, and employing the next generation of Palestinian men and women business and civic leaders. It builds the base of human capital for the Palestinian economy and prioritizes investment in technical and vocational education; science, technology, engineering, and mathematics (STEM) programs; and workforce development training to better prepare Palestinians for the jobs of today and the economy of tomorrow. Businesses will have a greater confidence that Palestinians will have the skills necessary to fill the jobs they seek to create, which will lead to a virtuous cycle of new investment and the expansion of existing operations.

ENTREPRENEURSHIP AND INNOVATION

Entrepreneurship, innovation, and private-sector growth are the cornerstones of vibrant economies. The recent success of Palestinian startups proves that Palestinian entrepreneurs have an impressive ability to build inventive, value-creating companies. To capitalize on their momentum, an institutional framework for growth should be adopted to position additional Palestinian entrepreneurs and companies for success. The incubator ecosystem in neighboring countries currently remains untapped by the Palestinian people, and Palestinians from around the world offer a talent pool that could support a strong, local startup culture. This program will support emerging Palestinian startups by helping Palestinian entrepreneurs overcome impediments to growth and break through the resource constraints they face today. Working in partnership with growing Palestinian and international venture capital firms, this project will incentivize regional cooperation for, and private investment in, promising Palestinian startups. Coupled with other investments in education and digital services, this program will help empower the next generation of Palestinian entrepreneurs to innovate and build their own successful companies, creating a successful entrepreneurial environment in the West Bank and Gaza.

SMALL AND MEDIUM BUSINESSES

Palestinian Micro, Small, and Medium Enterprises (MSMEs), which today employ a majority of the Palestinian labor force, are critical to the success of the Palestinian economy. A thriving domestic business sector in the West Bank and Gaza will require access to credit and reforms to core laws, rules, policies, and regulations that create barriers to business and stagnate private-sector growth. *Peace to Prosperity* will ensure that all Palestinians—not just the wealthy and connected— share in the benefits of peace. A robust local business sector will create good-paying, high-quality jobs for working-class Palestinians and is ultimately the key driver of prosperity. In order to promote a job-creating environment for the working class, this project will encourage the Palestinians to build a new commercial framework that includes all key elements of a thriving business sector and that nurtures small- and medium-business growth. This program will support loans to small businesses in the West Bank and Gaza to ensure that these enterprises have access to the capital needed to reinvest in their operations and in the growth of their companies. Support to small and medium businesses will spur the growth of local enterprises, which can serve as partners to large international companies seeking to do business or make foreign direct investment. Prioritizing the creation of an institutionalized pro-growth policy framework will end the vicious cycle of poverty plaguing the Palestinian people and begin a transformation toward sustainable development and prosperity.

UNLEASHING ECONOMIC POTENTIAL BY OPENING THE WEST BANK AND GAZA

ROADS AND RAIL

The Palestinian people routinely encounter logistical challenges in the West Bank and Gaza, impeding travel, stagnating economic growth, reducing exports, and stunting foreign direct investment. *Peace to Prosperity* presents an opportunity to physically integrate the Palestinian community through an efficient, modern transportation network. This project will support the construction of roads across the West Bank and Gaza. Additional investment will finance the development of a transportation corridor directly connecting the West Bank and Gaza through a major road and, potentially, a modern rail line. These improvements will reduce the complications of travel for Palestinians and remove impediments that delay or prevent goods from reaching end markets by directly connecting population centers and easing barriers to movement.

BORDER CROSSINGS

To sustain economic growth, Palestinian goods and people must be able to easily and securely move across borders. This project will provide financial and technical assistance to build the capacity of immigration and customs officials to operate and manage crossing points in coordination with neighboring states. This project will also upgrade facilities at key crossing points along borders and construct new ports of entry. Upgraded or newly constructed terminals will be equipped with the latest border crossing technology, and older terminals will be refurbished and improved with amenities for travelers to use while in transit. Ultimately, this project has the potential to unlock unprecedented levels of trade, grow exports, and increase foreign direct investment in the West Bank and Gaza and its neighbors—particularly Egypt, Israel, and Jordan.

> **> BREAKOUT VENTURE**

PROJECT:
"Breaking Down Barriers" Border Crossing Points Upgrades

LOCATION:
West Bank and Gaza

FINANCING:
Up to $900 million in grant funding

PROJECT OVERVIEW:
New cargo terminals, special access roads, and other infrastructure will be built at major crossing points. These funds will also support capacity-building programs to train Palestinian officials in best practices and to finance the deployment of new systems and technologies. These investments will reduce wait times and improve customer service at crossing points. The project will create hundreds of direct jobs in construction and crossing-point management and thousands of jobs across the Palestinian economy by reducing the costs of trade and travel.

UNLEASHING ECONOMIC POTENTIAL BY CONSTRUCTING ESSENTIAL INFRASTRUCTURE

POWER

The shortage of affordable electricity has had profound effects on the well-being of the Palestinian people, particularly in Gaza. In the near term, this project will focus on bringing the Gaza electricity crisis to a swift end—ensuring that Palestinians in Gaza receive at least 16 hours of electricity per day within a year of project implementation. This objective will be accomplished through investments in grid upgrades, the Gaza Power Plant, and new renewable energy facilities. Additional investments in energy infrastructure will ensure Gaza has continuous access to electricity within five years and will reduce the cost of electricity in the West Bank by increasing domestic supply and improving grid infrastructure. Finally, this project will provide technical support to increase the capacity of Palestinian utilities to manage and service this sector.

> BREAKOUT VENTURE

PROJECT:
"Power Gaza" Power Plant Upgrade

LOCATION:
Gaza

FINANCING:
Up to $590 million in grants and concessional financing

PROJECT OVERVIEW:
Stage One of this project will provide up to $90 million in grant funding to support the conversion of the Gaza Power Plant from diesel fuel to natural gas and connect it to a natural gas supply. This will increase electricity supply in Gaza by approximately 70 megawatts (MW) and significantly reduce the cost of electricity for Palestinians. In Stage Two, an additional investment of $500 million will expand the production capacity of the Gaza Power Plant by an additional 400 MW. The project will create hundreds of jobs in construction. It will also support the creation of thousands of jobs by supplying businesses in Gaza with reliable and affordable electricity for the first time in years.

WATER AND WASTEWATER

Access to water is a critical enabler of economic activity across many sectors of the Palestinian economy. By channeling significant investments into infrastructure that increases water supply, including desalination facilities, wells, and distribution networks, this project has the potential to double the amount of potable water available to Palestinians, per capita, within five years. Additional funding will support the development of new wastewater treatment facilities in the West Bank and Gaza, putting an end to the ongoing public-health risk posed by untreated wastewater. This treated water will be reused, creating vast supplies of affordable water for agricultural and industrial use.

DIGITAL SERVICES

While much of the world has experienced a digital technology revolution, digital services in the West Bank and Gaza are limited. This project will help the Palestinians leap a generation forward in digital services by providing financial incentives and technical expertise to support the Palestinian private sector in developing 4G LTE and 5G telecommunications services. To further expand internet access, other financial incentives will support Palestinian companies and municipalities in providing public high-speed wireless internet services. These investments will generate a digital transformation in the West Bank and Gaza and support economic growth across multiple sectors of the Palestinian economy.

UNLEASHING ECONOMIC POTENTIAL BY PROMOTING PRIVATE-SECTOR GROWTH

TOURISM

Unique and exciting characteristics give the West Bank and Gaza the potential to transform into a successful global tourism destination. Very few places in the world are home to such remarkable historical and religious sites. In addition, over forty kilometers of coastline in Gaza along the Mediterranean Sea could develop into a modern metropolitan city overlooking the beach, drawing from examples like **Beirut, Hong Kong, Lisbon, Rio de Janeiro, Singapore, and Tel Aviv.** Equally promising, traditional Palestinian cuisine varies across regions and excites visitors. Each Palestinian city boasts its own trademark dishes and flavors, from Ramallah's Rukab ice cream to the famed knafeh of Nablus. Together, these attractions endow the West Bank and Gaza with rich potential tourism opportunities. To unlock the benefits of increased tourism in the West Bank and Gaza, this project will support investment in hotels, food and beverage establishments, and other tourism-related industries. Additional funding will be used to improve hospitality training and to renovate and upgrade tourist sites. Finally, this project will also finance a major international marketing campaign to highlight tourism attractions in the West Bank and Gaza to audiences around the world. Through these and other investments, the Palestinians will gain access to the resources they need to build a thriving tourism industry—one with the potential to bring tens of thousands of visitors a year to the West Bank and Gaza and to stimulate economic growth across multiple sectors of the Palestinian economy.

> ❯ BREAKOUT VENTURE

PROJECT:
Tourism Lending Facility and Site Rehabilitation

LOCATION:
West Bank and Gaza

FINANCING:
Up to $750 million in concessional financing
Up to $200 million in grant funding

PROJECT OVERVIEW:
To fully develop the Palestinian tourism industry, new investments are needed to improve accommodations and attractions close to popular tourist sites. This project will provide hoteliers and tourism companies with access to low-interest loans through a new lending facility managed in conjunction with Palestinian banks. Up to $375 million of loan capacity will be available for the five-year life of the program, ensuring Palestinians have access to the capital required to quickly develop this sector. After five years, this facility could be extended and expanded for an additional five years. Separately, an additional $200 million in grant funding will support the rehabilitation and development of potential tourism sites.

AGRICULTURE

While agriculture accounts for approximately eight percent of Palestinian employment, this sector has not met its potential due to limited access of Palestinian farmers to land, water, and technology. An improved business environment in the West Bank and Gaza and access to more land will create an enormous opportunity for farmers to expand their operations.

At the same time, this project will support farmers who seek to secure financing from local banks and work with financial technology (FinTech) innovators. With increased access to capital, farmers will have the opportunity to purchase new seeds and fertilizers while developing greenhouses, irrigation systems, and other infrastructure. Other funding will help to rehabilitate arable land and build a new educational center to enhance agricultural education and training. These improvements will grow the capability of Palestinian farmers to shift their efforts to producing higher-value crops and afford them the opportunity to use modern farming techniques, further benefiting their businesses and, ultimately, their families.

HOUSING

High real estate prices across the West Bank and Gaza have made it difficult for many Palestinians to purchase a home. Peace will increase construction in the West Bank and Gaza and drive down property costs. The ability to access new housing stock, supported by mortgages from Palestinian banks to qualified homebuyers, will support a growing housing market, improve the quality of life for average Palestinians, and help build strong communities. As property rights strengthen, Palestinian homeowners also will be able to utilize their home assets as loan collateral, which may be used for small business borrowing or capital investment, further stimulating the Palestinian economy and increasing employment.

MANUFACTURING

From olive-wood carvings to exquisite embroidery, Palestinian craftsmanship has been in international demand for hundreds of years. Today, Palestinians have the opportunity to revive their legacy of high-quality manufacturing in the West Bank and Gaza. This program will support the development of state-of-the-art industrial zones and other manufacturing facilities in which Palestinian companies will benefit from tax and financing incentives that will lower the cost of doing business. Further, these specialized zones will provide companies with on-site services and training facilities in order to increase competitiveness and productivity. Part of the funding provided by this project will be dedicated to the development of joint facilities with neighboring countries, which will help enable the Palestinians and their neighbors to pool resources for their mutual benefit. Through this program, products made by Palestinians will be known for quality and value and have the potential fill the shelves of stores and warehouses around the world.

NATURAL RESOURCES

The West Bank and Gaza have significant endowments of stone and marble, hydrocarbons, and other minerals. This project will provide support for the development of major resource reserves, such as the Gaza Marine natural gas field, oil fields, and quarrying sites in the West Bank. It will also provide technical assistance to develop a regulatory framework for natural resource exploitation, including for shared resources along border areas. These resources have the potential to generate billions of dollars in revenue and create thousands of high-quality and good-paying Palestinian jobs.

UNLEASHING ECONOMIC POTENTIAL BY STRENGTHENING REGIONAL DEVELOPMENT AND INTEGRATION

ECONOMIC STABILIZATION AND DEVELOPMENT

The long-term economic outlook for the West Bank and Gaza is correlated to the economic strength and stability of neighboring countries. Presently, Egypt, Jordan, and Lebanon—important markets for the Palestinians—face distinct economic challenges. This project will draw upon these countries' national development plans to help them overcome obstacles to their economic growth by supporting efforts to provide reliable domestic electricity, improve water delivery, bolster private-sector businesses, strengthen financial institutions, and modernize public-sector services. These investments will reduce the risk of regional economic instability and create a significant opportunity for the Palestinians to increase exports, grow foreign direct investment, and build new business partnerships with companies in the region.

REGIONAL TRADE AND COMMERCE

Regional integration and cooperation have the potential to create significant new economic opportunities for the Palestinian people. Just as **Dubai and Singapore** have benefited from their strategic locations and flourished as regional financial hubs, the West Bank and Gaza can ultimately develop into a regional trading center. This project will encourage the construction of new infrastructure to facilitate trade and transportation across the West Bank and Gaza, Jordan, Egypt, Israel, and Lebanon. From the improvement of neighboring countries' airports and seaports to the development of a regional natural gas trading hub in Egypt, this project will improve mobility in the region and unlock new trade opportunities for the Palestinian private sector.

REGIONAL INVESTMENT

To improve the economic prospects of the region as a whole, attention must be devoted to igniting organic growth in the private sectors of neighboring countries. Drawing from the lessons of **Poland** in the 1990s and **Egypt** and **Tunisia** after the Arab Spring in 2011, enterprise funds have had proven success in promoting growth by using public-sector seed money for investment funds targeting private equity and credit. Jordan, and possibly Lebanon and others, could benefit tremendously from new enterprise funds that support domestic companies. Such funds could invest equity capital into early-stage, promising private-sector businesses in these countries, create tens of thousands of new direct and indirect jobs for their citizens, and facilitate partnerships with employees and their companies and experts in industries around the world. Successful new enterprise funds in the Middle East region would benefit the West Bank and Gaza, and could provide the basis for larger regional enterprise funds or a dedicated West Bank and Gaza enterprise fund in the future.

CROSS-BORDER SERVICES

From water pollution to electricity shortages, the countries of the region face many shared challenges. New developments along border areas between the West Bank and Gaza, Egypt, Israel, and Jordan can address many of these issues while generating new economic activity. This project will support the development of major wastewater treatment plants, desalination facilities, and power plants in and for this region. These improvements will provide necessary services to people in need, while also facilitating collaboration, integration, and cooperation between the governments of countries in the region.

REGIONAL TOURISM

The Palestinian tourism industry would benefit significantly from increased tourism activity in neighboring countries. Building on the appeal of attractions like the Egyptian Pyramids, the archaeological wonders of Petra in Jordan, and the beaches of Lebanon, the neighbors of West Bank and Gaza have immense potential to grow their tourism industries. This project will support private companies or public-private partnerships to develop tourism sites, transportation options, and hotel and restaurant accommodations across Egypt, Jordan, and Lebanon. In tandem with these investments, this project envisions that these countries, in collaboration with the Palestinians, will develop a cohesive regional tourism strategy, including shared investment plans, marketing campaigns, and regional tourism packages.

> ❯ BREAKOUT VENTURE

PROJECT:
Regional Tourism

LOCATION:
West Bank and Gaza, Egypt, Jordan, Lebanon

FINANCING:
Up to $1.5 billion in concessional financing
Up to $500 million in grants

PROJECT OVERVIEW:
With its culture, natural beauty, and historical and religious sites, the region has extraordinary tourism potential. This project will support private-sector domestic businesses and public-private partnerships to develop tourism sites and infrastructure in West Bank and Gaza, Egypt, Jordan, and Lebanon. Additional funding will be allocated to develop a regional-tourism strategy and marketing campaign focused on increasing the number of tourists that travel to multiple countries in the region within a single trip. These investments have the potential to increase tourism to the region as a whole and attract tens of thousands of additional tourists to the West Bank and Gaza each year.

## CHAPTER TWO

EMPOWERING THE PALESTINIAN PEOPLE

The greatest resource of every nation is its people.

The second initiative of *Peace to Prosperity* will unlock the vast potential of the Palestinian people by empowering them to pursue their goals and ambitions. This part of the vision will support the Palestinian people through four core programs.

The first program will **ENHANCE THE QUALITY OF THE EDUCATION SYSTEM** in the West Bank and Gaza and ensure that no Palestinian is disadvantaged by inadequate educational opportunity. This program will support the development and training of Palestinian educators while expanding access to educational opportunities to underserved communities and demographics. Other projects will help encourage educational reforms and innovation. By providing financial incentives to support the development of improved academic standards and curricula, this program will help turn the West Bank and Gaza into a center of educational excellence.

The second program will **STRENGTHEN WORKFORCE DEVELOPMENT PROGRAMS**, reducing unemployment rates and increasing the occupational mobility of the Palestinian workforce. By supporting apprenticeships, career counseling, and job placement services, this program will help ensure Palestinian youth are fully prepared to enter the job market and achieve their professional goals. Additional projects will help employed workers receive the training they need to enhance their skills or change careers. Ultimately, this program will ensure that all Palestinians have access to the tools they need to compete in the global economy and take full advantage of the opportunities offered by this vision.

The third program will provide new resources and incentives to **TRANSFORM THE PALESTINIAN HEALTHCARE SECTOR** and ensure the Palestinian people have access to the care they need within the West Bank and Gaza. This program will rapidly increase the capacity of Palestinian hospitals by ensuring that they have the supplies, medicines, vaccines, and equipment to provide top-quality care and protect against health emergencies. Other funds will help improve services and standards in Palestinian healthcare facilities. Through targeted investments in new facilities, educational opportunities for medical staff and aspiring healthcare professionals, and public awareness campaigns to improve preventative care, this program will significantly improve health outcomes throughout the West Bank and Gaza.

The fourth program will support projects that **IMPROVE THE QUALITY OF LIFE** for the Palestinian people. From investments in new cultural institutions to financial support for Palestinian artists and musicians, this program will help the next generation of Palestinians explore their creativity and hone their talents. It will also support improved municipal services and the development of new public spaces across the West Bank and Gaza. These developments will help turn the West Bank and Gaza into a cultural and recreational center to the benefit of all Palestinians.

EMPOWERING THE PALESTINIAN PEOPLE:
GOALS

> Boost human capital development in the West Bank and Gaza, achieving a 0.70 score on World Bank Human Capital Index

> Establish at least one Palestinian university in the global top 150

> Increase female labor force participation rate from 20 to 35 percent

> Reduce infant mortality from 18 to 9 per 1,000 births

> Increase average life expectancy from 74 to 80 years

EMPOWERING THE PALESTINIAN PEOPLE BY
ENHANCING EDUCATION SERVICES

EDUCATIONAL QUALITY

From Birzeit to Bethlehem, strong academic programs exist in the West Bank and Gaza to educate Palestinians, yet the quality of education varies widely between institutions. This project will enhance educational quality and consistency throughout the West Bank and Gaza by focusing on educational outcomes. It will also provide financial incentives to public and private Palestinian academic institutions to meet certain benchmarks, such as raising standards, improving curricula, and increasing post-graduation employment rates. In addition, expanding pre-service and in-service teacher training and certification opportunities will help ensure Palestinian teachers have the tools they need to help the next generation of Palestinians realize their full potential. Finally, this project will identify financial awards to recognize the accomplishments of Palestinian teachers and educational administrators who demonstrate success as measured by adopted metrics and standards.

> BREAKOUT VENTURE

PROJECT:
New Palestinian University

LOCATION:
West Bank and Gaza

FINANCING:
Up to $500 million in grants

PROJECT OVERVIEW:
To prepare Palestinian students to join the workforce of the 21st century, this project envisions the construction and development of a new flagship liberal arts and sciences university in the West Bank and Gaza. The project will incorporate input from Palestinian academic leaders to construct facilities that use the latest technology to deliver the highest-quality education. Top teachers and administrators will be recruited to impact the lives of Palestinians who are eager to learn and succeed academically. This project will also develop partnerships between the new university and top institutions abroad, which will incentivize academic exchanges and distance learning programs for Palestinian students and teachers. A separate Educational Affordability program will help ensure this university remains accessible to the general Palestinian public.

EDUCATIONAL ACCESS

While Palestinians have among the highest graduation rates in the region, many Palestinian schools are stretched beyond their capacity, with too few teachers and classrooms to support their students. To ensure all Palestinians have access to quality education, priority will be placed on expanding the capacity of early childhood, primary, and secondary schools, with a focus on supporting schools operating in underserved communities. This project will enable schools to expand their infrastructure and hire new teachers. To improve higher education, this project will support the creation of a new university in the West Bank and Gaza. Modeled after successful initiatives in the **United Arab Emirates and Qatar**, this new landmark institution will provide Palestinian students with direct access to a top international institution without leaving home.

EDUCATIONAL AFFORDABILITY

Like many students around the world, young Palestinians often encounter financial constraints that limit their educational opportunities. This project will reduce the financial burden on Palestinian students by expanding the resources available to finance their education. *Peace to Prosperity* will support a scholarship program whereby colleges and universities from around the world are encouraged to provide full and partial scholarships for Palestinian students to study abroad and obtain a world-class education. Palestinian banks will be offered technical assistance to support responsible student-lending, which will provide Palestinians options to supplement their scholarships and enroll in a quality academic program. Following graduation, these students would be expected to return home, as is typical in other countries with similar programs, to become a core element of the future generation of leaders in the West Bank and Gaza.

EMPOWERING THE PALESTINIAN PEOPLE BY STRENGTHENING WORKFORCE DEVELOPMENT

YOUTH AND WOMEN

Whether for a recent female tech graduate or a craftsman with 20 years of experience, building a brighter future in the West Bank and Gaza will require the contributions of all Palestinians. Unfortunately, Palestinians currently experience one of the highest youth-unemployment rates in the world. Equally problematic, while Palestinian women achieve higher levels of educational attainment than Palestinian men, Palestinian women constitute only a small percentage of the Palestinian workforce. By providing the Palestinian public sector with policy advice on best practices, encouraging private-sector attention to this problem, and promoting a comprehensive strategy to empower youth and women, more women and youth will join the Palestinian labor force. *Peace to Prosperity* envisions a West Bank and Gaza where youth and women become entrepreneurs and business owners, have access to capital, and learn the skills needed to succeed. This project will increase job placement rates for Palestinian youth and women by providing them with career counseling, specialized training, and job placement services in a concentrated effort to employ them in higher-wage, high-growth occupations.

> ❯ BREAKOUT VENTURE

PROJECT:
Career Counseling and
Job Placement

LOCATION:
West Bank and Gaza

FINANCING:
Up to $30 million in grants

PROJECT OVERVIEW:
Peace to Prosperity envisions women within the West Bank and Gaza receiving the financing, market opportunities, and workforce training to succeed as entrepreneurs and private businessowners. As a part of promoting the adoption of a comprehensive strategy to advance economic opportunities for women, this project will support the development of a central institution to facilitate career counseling and job-placement services for women and young Palestinians throughout the West Bank and Gaza. This institution will be connected to Palestinian universities and local chambers of commerce to coordinate with career services centers and recommend curriculum improvements. It will also serve as a job portal, providing Palestinian youth and women access to listings for potential jobs, as well as resume guidance and other services.

SCIENCE, TECHNOLOGY, ENGINEERING, AND MATHEMATICS

For hundreds of years, the Arab world was the global center of science and mathematics. But, in modern times, neither the West Bank nor Gaza has kept pace with the leaders in these fields. *Peace to Prosperity* will support the Palestinian scientific community by generating research and employment opportunities in the West Bank and Gaza. This program will sponsor research and development partnerships between Palestinian and international companies and global research institutions, while also encouraging international firms to partner with Palestinians in the development of new commercial technologies and scientific research. Those efforts should create many more opportunities for Palestinian science, technology, engineering, and mathematics (STEM) students.

TECHNICAL AND VOCATIONAL EDUCATION

From students who graduate without the training and skills to perform the jobs companies need, to employers who seek well-taught, workforce-ready employees, more and better technical and vocational education is both sought and needed in the West Bank and Gaza. Drawing from successful models such as those deployed in **Germany and Sweden**, and using the tools of community college and distance-learning programs, this project expands overall enrollment capacity in technical and vocational institutions and tailors educational training to improve marketability and employability for students. This project also supports the development of new partnerships between these institutions and Palestinian companies to ensure students coming out of school have a relevant knowledge of the workplace, a better understanding of employers' expectations, and a higher likelihood of success entering the workforce.

INTERNSHIPS AND APPRENTICESHIPS

Peace to Prosperity seeks to expand opportunities for on-the-job training and pre-graduation work experience for Palestinian students, with a particular focus on STEM fields. By partnering with the Palestinian public sector, the private sector, and non-profit organizations to develop new internship and apprenticeship programs for Palestinian students, this program will help Palestinian students gain work experience, identify gaps in their skill sets, and adjust their coursework accordingly. The goal of this project is to ensure that all Palestinians enrolled in universities and vocational schools have opportunities to intern or train at an institution that matches with their career goals, thereby increasing the likelihood they develop the skills needed for the jobs of the future and secure post-graduation gainful employment.

WORKFORCE TRAINING

To improve productivity and occupational mobility, employed Palestinians need access to training and educational opportunities that will help them develop new skills and advance their careers. This project will provide financial incentives to private-sector companies to develop training centers for their employees. These new facilities will be housed within industrial zones, which will be areas within the West Bank and Gaza designed to encourage investment and employment through preferential tax treatment. This project will also support Palestinians seeking to change careers by providing scholarships and fellowships to empower them to pursue new training and educational opportunities in Palestinian universities and vocational schools.

EMPOWERING THE PALESTINIAN PEOPLE BY INVESTING IN HEALTHCARE

HEALTHCARE ACCESS

Deficiencies of staff, medicine, equipment, and supplies in Palestinian medical facilities cause gaps in the Palestinian healthcare system and force many Palestinians to forgo care or travel abroad to receive the care they need. In the near term, this project will support the deployment of more mobile and neighborhood clinics to meet the healthcare needs of underserved Palestinian communities and provide financial support to ensure hospitals and clinics receive medicine and equipment to improve treatment for those most in need of care. Other, later-stage projects will outfit public hospitals with new, state-of-the-art equipment to improve their ability to treat a variety of ailments and diseases—reducing both wait times and the number of Palestinians that must be referred to hospitals abroad for treatment.

❯ BREAKOUT VENTURE

PROJECT:
Strengthening Palestinian Hospitals and Clinics

LOCATION:
West Bank and Gaza

FINANCING:
Up to $300 million in grant funding
Up to $600 million in concessional financing

PROJECT OVERVIEW:
The Palestinian healthcare system requires better medical facilities to enhance treatment capabilities. This project envisions the development of new private specialized treatment centers, ensuring Palestinians are able to receive quality treatment for a wide range of illnesses and conditions within the West Bank and Gaza, while partnering with Palestinian health offcials to focus on cost-control and afordability reforms.

HEALTHCARE QUALITY

The shortage of resources within the Palestinian healthcare system has made it challenging for healthcare professionals to fully focus on improving quality standards and for Palestinian medical institutions to meet the highest standards and achieve international accreditation. This project will support technical and private-sector experts assisting hospitals and clinics in identifying areas for improvement and provide them with the resources to address existing needs. To further improve quality of care, this project will encourage doctors, nurses, and other medical staff to pursue international certifications, trainings, and research opportunities. These skilled professionals and modernized facilities can provide the foundation for the long-term quality of healthcare in the West Bank and Gaza.

PREVENTIVE HEALTHCARE

The threat of non-communicable diseases in the West Bank and Gaza is growing and made worse by the lack of primary and secondary prevention programs. This project will help Palestinian healthcare facilities expand the availability of services like vaccines, family-health-history assessments, and regular physical and mental-health checkups. This project will also finance a public-awareness campaign to inform the people about healthcare risks and the resources available to them within the Palestinian healthcare system. These efforts will reduce long-term healthcare costs and help the Palestinian people lead longer, healthier lives.

EMPOWERING THE PALESTINIAN PEOPLE BY IMPROVING QUALITY OF LIFE

ARTS AND CULTURE

From ancient to modern times, the West Bank and Gaza have been a center of arts and culture. They are home to many of the region's most renowned artists and poets and are steeped in historic traditions, like the annual Nabi Musa festival. This great cultural legacy should be celebrated and supported. Working with Palestinian cultural institutions, this project will lift up the next generation of great Palestinian artists, musicians, and writers. Palestinians will have the opportunity to apply for year-long fellowships to study, train, and work in artistic and cultural fields at home and abroad. Other grants will finance the development of new cultural centers and museums across the West Bank and Gaza. These institutions will showcase the richness of Palestinian history and culture for thousands of local and international visitors each day.

SPORTS AND ATHLETICS

In addition to improving public health, sports and athletics can help Palestinian youth foster new ties with their peers and within their communities, and Palestinian teams can be a source of entertainment and pride for all Palestinians. This project will expand options for competitive, healthy activities for Palestinians through the construction of public athletic facilities in the West Bank and Gaza. This project seeks to inspire the next generation of Palestinian athletes dreaming to be on, and training for, future Palestinian teams competing on the world stage.

> ❯ BREAKOUT VENTURE

PROJECT:
Urban Renewal

LOCATION:
West Bank and Gaza

FINANCING:
Up to $200 million in grant funding

PROJECT OVERVIEW:
Working with top Palestinian urban planners, this project will assist Palestinian municipalities in developing and rehabilitating infrastructure which will improve the quality of life within Palestinian urban areas. These funds will finance the development of sidewalks, libraries, parks, and other public spaces in cities and towns. They will also support the renovation of public buildings and other revitalization projects that beautify and improve urban areas across the West Bank and Gaza.

MUNICIPAL SERVICES

Palestinian municipalities lack the resources to deliver the basic services their citizens require to thrive. This project will improve services in Palestinian cities and towns by providing short-term funding to municipalities and non-governmental organizations focused on improving the lives of local citizens. These funds will allow local governments and institutions to improve basic services, including trash collection, emergency assistance, and traffic management. This funding will be linked to a series of reforms that will put Palestinian municipalities on a path toward independently funding and sustainably providing public services. Other funding will support the development of public spaces across the West Bank and Gaza, giving Palestinians more opportunities to spend time outdoors with their families and friends while also helping attract tourism to the West Bank and Gaza.

## CHAPTER THREE

ENHANCING PALESTINIAN GOVERNANCE

While implementing Peace to Prosperity will require significant international support, no vision for the Palestinians can be realized without the full support of the Palestinian people and their leadership.

The third and final initiative of *Peace to Prosperity* seeks to encourage the Palestinian public sector to provide the services and administration necessary for the Palestinian people to have a better future. If the government realizes its potential by investing in its people and adopting the foundational elements identified in *Peace to Prosperity*, job growth will ensue and the Palestinian people and their economy will thrive. This vision establishes a path that, in partnership with the Palestinian public sector, will enable prosperity through three programs.

The first program of this initiative will help the Palestinian public sector **TRANSFORM THE BUSINESS ENVIRONMENT** through private property rights; safeguards against corruption; access to credit; functioning capital markets along with pro-growth policies and regulations; and certainty and predictability for investors that result in economic growth, private-sector job creation, and increased exports and foreign direct investment. Just as the **Japanese, South Korean, and Singaporean** governments rose to meet the daunting challenges their societies faced at critical times in their respective histories, so too can the Palestinian leadership chart a new course for its people. This program identifies and addresses the requirements for developing human capital, igniting innovation, creating and growing small and medium businesses, and attracting international companies that will invest in the future of the West Bank and Gaza.

The second program will invest in projects that **BUILD THE INSTITUTIONS** of the Palestinian public sector and enhance government responsiveness to the people. Through this program, government attention will be directed to increase judicial independence and grow civil society organizations. A stronger court system will better protect and secure the rights and property of the citizens. More government transparency will help foster trust from Palestinians—and outside investors—that court decisions are made fairly, contracts are awarded and enforced honestly, and business investments are safe.

The final program will **IMPROVE GOVERNMENT OPERATIONS** and the provision of services to the Palestinian people. In line with successful private-sector models, the Palestinian public sector must strive to be fiscally stable, financially independent, caring to its workers, and efficient in providing services to its citizens. This program will work to eliminate public-sector arrears and implement a budgeting and tax plan that promotes long-term fiscal sustainability, without the need for budget support or donor funds. It will also assist with the adoption of new technologies that can provide Palestinian citizens the ability to directly request and access government support and services. The program will offer new training and opportunities for civil servants to improve their productivity, help prepare them to meet governance challenges, and make it easier for them to perform their jobs. And, finally, this program aims to provide government services at low cost and high efficiency, which will facilitate private-sector growth.

ENHANCING PALESTINIAN GOVERNANCE:

GOALS

> Improve government transparency, achieving a Transparency International Corruption Perceptions Index score of 60 or better

> Implement an e-government system, achieving a United Nations E-Government Development Index score greater than 0.75

> Enact a sustainable public-sector budget

> Enhance the business environment, achieving a World Bank Doing Business ranking of 75 or better

ENHANCING PALESTINIAN GOVERNANCE BY CREATING A BETTER BUSINESS ENVIRONMENT

PROPERTY RIGHTS

Private property rights and legal protections for business owners are prerequisites for sustainable economic development. Through this program, the Palestinian public sector will receive assistance in creating and improving the legal frameworks that advance systems of commercial law, competition law, bankruptcy law, and contract law. This program will work with the Palestinian public sector to clearly define private property rights, develop institutional protections for property owners, and register land ownership in a national database. Land registration is a critical step in the transformation of the Palestinian economy, which will unlock property for use as collateral for capital and eliminate many existing barriers to development. Ultimately, *Peace to Prosperity* envisions Palestinians having the opportunity to develop and modernize cities, villages, industrial areas, and agricultural lands, potentially generating billions of dollars in new economic activity. Strong property rights are critical to realizing this future.

LEGAL AND TAX FRAMEWORK

Long-term economic growth requires a legal and tax framework that supports the private sector and attracts investment. This project will provide technical and financial assistance to the Palestinian public sector to transition toward a pro-growth tax structure, install improved anti-corruption measures, open capital markets, and develop regulatory reforms that support economic growth. By developing new laws and regulations that increase competition, protect intellectual property and contract rights, and ensure legal recourse, this project will help give businesses the confidence they need to make new investments and expand existing operations. This project will also support ongoing efforts to develop a one-stop-shop for Palestinian business registration, which could dramatically reduce the cost and time required to start a company. These reforms will help ensure all Palestinians—not just major corporations—are able to take full advantage of the opportunities created by this vision.

> ❯ BREAKOUT VENTURE

PROJECT:
Land Registration

LOCATION:
West Bank and Gaza

FINANCING:
Up to $30 million in grant funding

PROJECT OVERVIEW:
This program will help Palestinian property owners quickly register their land assets in a single database. Implemented in partnership with development institutions and the Palestinian public sector, it will help resolve contested land ownership claims and clearly define private property rights. Reinforcing private property rights provides the security necessary for productive investments, while ensuring that owners are able to gain access to capital by mortgaging or selling their property.

CAPITAL MARKETS AND MONETARY POLICY

The Palestinian financial sector will be a critical partner in the implementation of *Peace to Prosperity*. This program will bolster the capacity of the financial authorities and private sector Palestinian banks to promote the health of the domestic financial system while facilitating an increase in productive lending, particularly to small and medium businesses. Palestinian banking authorities must be able to work with domestic banks to expand their capabilities to support a growing Palestinian business sector and to be effective channels for foreign investment and capital flows. Specifically, technical assistance will support efforts to preserve correspondent banking relations, optimize bank-lending practices, and build the capacity of financial authorities to regulate the banking sector and manage a portfolio of securities.

INTERNATIONAL TRADE AND FOREIGN DIRECT INVESTMENT

In addition to infrastructure expansion, increasing Palestinian exports will require the development of new trade policies. Under this program, robust technical support will help the applicable Palestinian authorities to establish a fair and reciprocal trade regime, manage commercial crossing points, and implement regulatory reforms that attract new trading partners. In parallel with these efforts, this project will bring multinational corporate leaders to the West Bank and Gaza and facilitate international investor conferences that raise awareness of opportunities to partner with, and invest in, Palestinian companies. Technical experts will also work with Palestinian officials to help them develop beneficial free trade agreements. Expanded Palestinian regional and international trade will be central to the long-term growth of the Palestinian economy, and a focus on Palestinian exports will compel domestic companies to increase efficiency and quality to compete successfully in international markets.

ENHANCING PALESTINIAN GOVERNANCE
THROUGH INSTITUTION BUILDING

JUDICIAL INDEPENDENCE

In accord with the principles of rule of law and separation of powers, the independence of the Palestinian judicial branch must be reassessed and strengthened. A strong judiciary and reliable court system allow businesses to know that their investments will be secure and that their companies and the products they create will be protected from unfair treatment. Confidence in legal matters is a critical element of business risk reduction, which attracts private capital and foreign investment. To this end, this project will partner with the Palestinian authorities to encourage laws and regulations that secure the independence of the judicial system. It will invest in building the capacity of the courts, with a particular focus on enhancing their ability to handle cases covering potential government abuse. In addition, this program will promote legal education, which will, among other things, help leaders better identify legal and regulatory reforms that would improve the government procurement process and the overall business environment.

PROJECT:
Palestinian E-Governance

LOCATION:
West Bank and Gaza

FINANCING:
Up to $300 million in grant funding

PROJECT OVERVIEW:
This project will fund the development of a central online e-government system. Modeled after similar systems implemented in countries like Estonia, this portal will empower government ministries and everyday Palestinian citizens to share information and communicate in real time. Through this system, Palestinians will be able to request information from public-sector institutions regarding decisions and policies. This system will also allow Palestinians to request public-sector services, as discussed in the Service Delivery project.

ACCOUNTABILITY

Good governance requires rigorous systems that empower people to hold institutions accountable. Palestinians contribute tax revenue with the expectation that their government will spend it responsibly to provide services efficiently and effectively. Palestinians should have more and better avenues to seek accountability for allegations of government waste, fraud, and abuse; episodes of government corruption; instances of unfair or atypical decisions in criminal cases; and unnecessary obstacles to the creation or growth of a business. In order for the Palestinian people to build confidence in their government, they need mechanisms to express their concerns and see actions in response. This project will enhance the capacity of Palestinian anti-corruption institutions, including their capability to investigate allegations of corruption and mismanagement and to refer findings to competent domestic authorities without interference. This program will also provide technical and financial assistance to expand the capacity of the internal government auditor—empowering it to review public-sector expenditures and investigate anomalies in a timely and transparent manner.

TRANSPARENCY

For the people to hold their government accountable, government policy decisions, the legislative process, and public-sector actions regarding procurement, contracts, licenses, and hiring need to be transparent. Palestinians should know how their government spends taxpayer money, and the government can improve its performance by making better use of the internet and digital platforms. New technologies have allowed and encouraged governments worldwide to improve transparency and accountability measures to the benefit of their citizens. This project will support the Palestinian institutions in adopting enhancements that improve public-sector transparency and communication directly with the Palestinian people. In order to sustain a future of prosperity, the Palestinian leadership owes its people a commitment to transparent governance, which inspires confidence in a bright future of opportunity.

CIVIL SOCIETY

Robust civil society institutions and a free press are important parts of any well-functioning democracy. Preserving and expanding these important institutions within the West Bank and Gaza will require new laws and practices that protect their independence and improve their capacity. To support these efforts, this project will provide training to Palestinian officials to help them enhance protections for civil society and ensure the freedom of the press. It will also support civil society organizations by identifying the resources needed to perform their important functions.

ENHANCING PALESTINIAN GOVERNANCE BY
IMPROVING GOVERNMENT OPERATIONS

FISCAL SUSTAINABILITY

To promote the long-term health of the Palestinian economy, the Palestinian public sector must have a fiscally-sustainable budget. Under this project, technical experts will advise the Palestinian financial authorities on developing a plan to put the government on a path towards fiscal sustainability, with focuses on ending reliance on donor aid, efficiently raising domestic tax revenue, and increasing capacity to manage a portfolio of government securities. To support this effort, this project will provide short-term financial support to the Palestinian public sector to pay off its arrears to the private sector. It will support the deployment of new systems that build in accountability and transparency and that enable the applicable Palestinian authorities to manage revenue collection at all commercial crossings and other ports of entry. The project will require the Palestinian public sector to implement systems that improve the efficiency, accountability, and transparency of payment collections for services such as electricity and water, which will help to reduce the long-term costs for consumers and encourage private investment.

❯ BREAKOUT VENTURE

PROJECT:
Attracting Global Expertise

LOCATION:
West Bank and Gaza

FINANCING:
Up to $100 million in grant funding

PROJECT OVERVIEW:
The Palestinian diaspora offers a tremendous potential source of talent for the Palestinian economy. Peace to Prosperity will require a significant increase in human capital capacity, and this project will support efforts to bring together and empower talented Palestinians and other experts from around the world to implement it.

CIVIL SERVICE

Good Palestinian governance requires commitment to its customers: the Palestinian people. Government's core missions, top goals, and strategic objectives should be developed and aligned to increase the prosperity of the citizenry. To improve the quality of government employees in the West Bank and Gaza, this project will support the development of new educational programs and leadership training for civil servants, with a rigorous curriculum that focuses on being responsive to the needs of the people and providing excellent customer service. These programs will provide the next generation of Palestinian officials with skills in leadership, teamwork, negotiations, financial management, policy-making, and communications, while also promoting a culture of service and accountability. Performance metrics will be identified and career advancement will be rewarded based on measurable results. Leaders will learn to identify, prioritize, and showcase the government's most important goals—and metrics for those goals—to best produce outcomes that will improve life in the West Bank and Gaza and grow the economy. Progress against baselines will be measured, tracked, and produced on the internet for the citizens to hold their government accountable for success. Measurements for growth in exports, foreign direct investment, and job growth are examples of metrics that can easily be evaluated and published.

SERVICE DELIVERY

A revitalized Palestinian economy will require modernized Palestinian public-sector services and institutions. This project will assist the applicable Palestinian authorities in implementing a comprehensive strategy to ensure the efficient delivery of services to its people. This effort will expand online government services, including payment services, utility management, school registration, and passport applications. These same systems will allow Palestinians to track the status of their requests and other performance indicators. To further boost the delivery of services, this project will work with the government to identify opportunities for public-private partnerships and to privatize services for which the private sector has a stronger, proven performance record.

Peace to Prosperity lays out a vision for a prosperous Palestinian society supported by a robust private sector, an empowered people, and an effective government. It shows what is possible with peace plus investment, and how success is achievable through specific programs supported by a portfolio of realizable projects.

Peace to Prosperity is a realistic and achievable plan that can be implemented by the Palestinians, with the support of the international community, to build a better future for the Palestinians and their children. Through this vision, the West Bank and Gaza can provide a future of dignity and opportunity for the Palestinian people.

APPENDIX 3

ECONOMIC INCENTIVE / ECONOMIC PACKAGE

A VISION FOR PALESTINIANS AND THE REGION

SUMMARY OVERVIEW

To transform and improve the lives of
the Palestinians and the people of the
region by unleashing economic
growth, unlocking human potential,
and enhancing Palestinian governance
following a peace agreement.

A VISION FOR PALESTINIANS AND THE MIDDLE EAST REGION

A Thriving and Integrated Economy

An Empowered and Prosperous People

An Accountable and Agile Government

THE VISION IS FOUNDED ON THREE TENETS

01   Unleashing Economic Potential

02   Empowering the Palestinian People

03   Enhancing Palestinian Governance

Peace to Prosperity is a vision to empower the Palestinian people to build a prosperous and vibrant Palestinian society. It consists of three initiatives that will support distinct pillars of the Palestinian society: the economy, the people, and the government. With the potential to facilitate more than $50 billion in new investment over ten years, Peace to Prosperity represents the most ambitious and comprehensive international effort for the Palestinians to date. The projects are drawn from private sector proposals, government planning documents, independent analysis, and the work of previous studies from organizations such as the World Bank Group, the International Monetary Fund, the Office of the Quartet, and others.

This document provides further information on the portfolio of projects, including brief descriptions, timelines, project financing estimates, and expected funding distribution by sector. The Peace to Prosperity Master Fund (the "Fund") will manage the financial and project support for these investments. The Fund will serve several essential functions.

First, it will act as a conduit for private businesses to have access to capital. Second, it will manage and sign-off on disbursement of funds by tranche, linked to achieving developmental milestones, which will be separately agreed to by the parties as conditions precedent to continuance of the economic plan. Third, it will be responsible for the transparency and accountability of disbursed funds, on behalf of donors, investors, and the Palestinian people.

Aiming to utilize an implementation mechanism analogous to that of the Marshall Plan—with a core focus on creating a thriving business sector and ending reliance on donor aid—the Fund will not be the implementing agent for the envisioned projects. Instead, independent businesses will predominately implement the projects. The prospective implementing parties will submit competitive project proposals, in many cases derived from existing commercial or public-sector plans. The Fund will also provide access to capital for projects not specifically outlined herein, particularly in support of entrepreneurs and small and medium businesses.

These programs are designed to use market principles and actors to underpin a 10-year plan for all key segments of the Palestinian economy, and provide the foundation for prosperity supported by a robust private sector, an empowered people, and an effective government. Peace to Prosperity is a realistic and achievable plan that can be implemented by the Palestinians, with the support of the international community, to build a better future for the Palestinians and their children. This vision can ensure a future of dignity and opportunity for the Palestinian people.

HIGH LEVEL GOALS

WITHIN 10 YEARS

01 More than double Palestinian gross domestic product

02 Create over one million Palestinian jobs

03 Reduce the Palestinian unemployment rate to nearly single digits

04 Reduce the Palestinian poverty rate by 50 percent

WEST BANK / GAZA PROGRAM TOTALS

(US$ in m m)

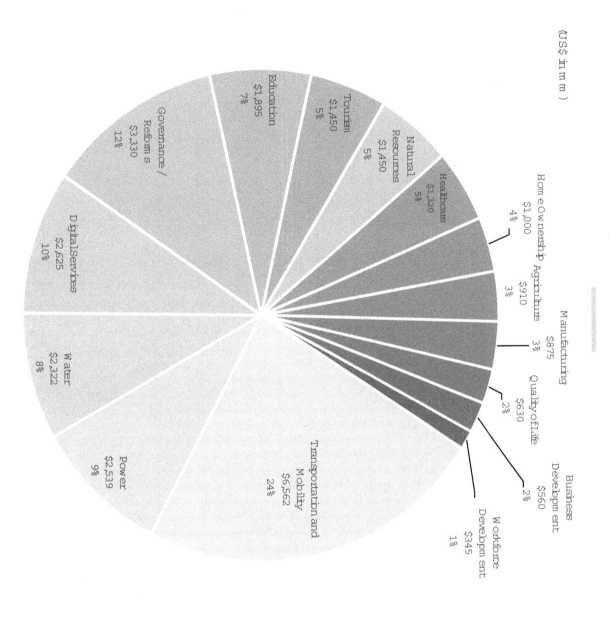

Home Ownership
$1,000
4%

Agriculture
$910
3%

Manufacturing
$875
3%

Quality of Life
$630
2%

Business
Development
$560
2%

Workforce
Development
$345
1%

Transportation and
Mobility
$6,562
24%

Power
$2,539
9%

Water
$2,322
8%

Digital Services
$2,625
10%

Governance /
Reforms
$3,330
12%

Education
$1,895
7%

Tourism
$1,450
5%

Natural
Resources
$1,450
5%

Healthcare
$1,320
5%

REGIONAL PROGRAM TOTALS

(US$ in m m)

Gaza and W estBank
$27,813

Jordan
$7,365

Egypt
$9,167

Lebanon
$6,325

REGIONAL PROGRAM SUMMARY

!"#$%&'()*'+,	&'(#)	!"#$%		
		*+,	/+0	1+2	3+*4
!"#$%&	'()*+,	')*+-	')*+,	'(*.//	'.0(
123&45&75&9: #$&	-;*/+.	-*,0,	0*,;;	/*(-, |)*,+.
!"#$%&#$5&9: #$&	').*0,	';*);(	'(,*.*)0	'+*,+/	'<*,/(
="#$7&#@&#A	((*/,,	+;0	)*/.	-*;/-	(*/,-
B:%#AL:2"C7&	';,*/0,	'/*,+	'(<*,/	'()*+<<	';*/)

MACROECONOMIC IMPACT

	Base Year	Phase 1					Phase 2			Phase 3	
		Year1	Year2	Year3	Year4	Year5	Year6	Year7	Year8	Year9	Year10
GDP ($BN)	$14.6	$16.0	$17.6	$19.1	$20.7	$22.4	$24.2	$26.2	$28.3	$30.6	$33.1
GDP Growth Rate	-	9.8%	9.9%	8.3%	8.4%	8.4%	8.1%	8.1%	8.1%	8.1%	8.1%
GDP Per Capita ($)	$2,952	$3,171	$3,369	$3,524	$3,681	$3,846	$4,009	$4,179	$4,358	$4,546	$4,743
Total Jobs	1,050,756	1,153,499	1,267,278	1,372,953	1,487,639	1,612,126	1,742,139	1,882,718	2,034,729	2,199,108	2,376,868
New Jobs Created - Annual	-	102,743	113,779	105,674	114,687	124,487	130,012	140,579	152,011	164,379	177,760
New Jobs Created - Cumulative	-	102,743	216,522	322,197	436,883	561,370	691,382	831,962	983,973	1,148,352	1,326,112
Unemployment Rate	30.9%	26.4%	27.3%	23.2%	24.0%	20.0%	20.5%	16.5%	16.6%	12.6%	12.4%

Key Statistics	
Total New Jobs Created	1,326,111
Total GDP Increase (%)	126.7%
Compound Annual GDP Growth Rate (%)	8.5%
Total GDP Per Capita Increase (%)	60.7%
Unemployment	12.4%

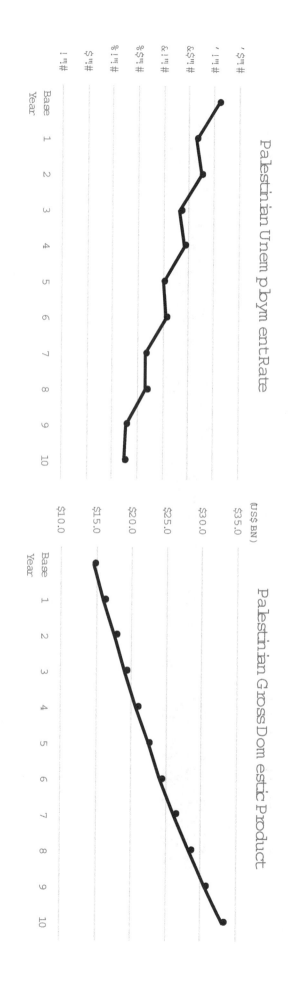

Palestinian Unemployment Rate

Palestinian Gross Domestic Product

UNLEASHING ECONOMIC POTENTIAL

## CHAPTER ONE

Thriving
& Integrated
Economy

Empowered
& Prosperous
People

Accountable
& Agile
Government

1
UNLEASHING
ECONOMIC
POTENTIAL

Building a Foundation
for Growth and Business
Investment

Opening the West Bank
and Gaza

Constructing Essential
Infrastructure

Promoting Private
Sector Growth

Strengthening
Regional Development
and Integration

BUILDING A FOUNDATION FOR GROWTH AND BUSINESS INVESTMENT

Generating rapid growth and job creation through a new institutional foundation for the Palestinian economy.

GOALS

Achieve a World Bank Doing Business ranking of 75 or better

Building a Foundation for Growth and Business Investment

Strategy for Reform

Human Capital

Entrepreneurship and Innovation

Small and Medium Businesses

BUILDING A FOUNDATION FOR GROWTH AND BUSINESS INVESTMENT

STRATEGY FOR REFORM

US$ in mm unless otherwise specified

#	Project	Description	Phase	Total Est. Cost	Grants	Concessional Loans	Private	Implementation Timeline
1	Property Ownership Resolution	Enhance court capacity to quickly and effectively resolve property disputes and contested-ownership claims.	1	$60	$60	–	–	3 years; 50 percent within 1 year, the remainder within 3 years
2	Business Registration	Build an efficient, one-stop-shop for business registration and other resources for business owners.	1	50	50	–	–	1 year
3	New Laws and Reforms	Provide technical assistance to streamline regulations across all sectors to excite economic growth. Some priorities may include (but will not be limited to) the implementation of commercial, competition, investment promotion, intellectual property, and public-private partnership laws, with an emphasis on the implementation of an efficient and low-burden tax system.	1	50	50	–	–	3 years
4	Technical Assistance for the Financial Sector and Regulators	Provide technical assistance for Palestinian financial institutions and the Palestinian financial sector to support best lending practices and appropriately expand access to capital for underserved sectors and demographics.	1	25	25	–	–	2 years
5	Technical Support for Customs/Trade Functions	Provide training to build the capacity of the Palestinian public sector to manage crossing points, inspect goods, and facilitate trade, with an emphasis on the implementation of anti-corruption safeguards.	1	50	50	–	–	2 years
6	Technical Support to Develop Palestinian Trade Policy	Provide robust technical support to the Palestinian public sector to develop a new trade regime and framework that works best for the Palestinian people.	1	25	25	–	–	2 years
7	Enhancing Anti-Corruption Bodies	Provide technical assistance and training to build the capacity of the anti-corruption authorities.	1	25	25	–	–	3 years

Projects listed under this section may appear under other program areas below. The Strategy for Reform program was designed to highlight how projects under the "Empowering the People" and "Enhancing Governance" initiatives will directly improve the business environment in the West Bank and Gaza and pave the way for increased investment.

BUILDING A FOUNDATION FOR GROWTH AND BUSINESS INVESTMENT

STRATEGY FOR REFORM

(US$ in mm unless otherwise specified)

	Project	Description	Phase	Total Est. Cost	Financing Grants	Concessional Loans	Private	Implementation Timeline
8	Improving Internal Auditing Capabilities	Develop the capacity of the public sector audit and administrative controls institution to audit public-sector expenditures and conduct investigations.	1	25	25	-	-	3 years
9	Institutional Reforms	Provide technical support to develop standardized and transparent processes and procedures for human resources and regulatory reviews, in areas such as license issuance.	1	25	25	-	-	3 years
10	Increasing Revenue Collection Efficiency	Invest in new systems that will allow the Palestinian public sector to manage and monitor the collection of revenues at commercial crossing points.	1	25	25	-	-	3 years
11	Managing Expenditures	Provide technical assistance to help the Palestinian public sector evaluate its expenditures and budgetary processes and identify potential efficiencies.	1	25	25	-	-	3 years
12	Procurement management	Standardize efficient and accountable processes for Palestinian public-sector procurement decisions, with an emphasis on the implementation of anti-corruption safeguards.	1	25	25	-	-	3 years
13	Public-Private Partnerships	Identify services and utilities that could be provided by the private sector to improve efficiency and reduce costs, particularly in areas of service delivery, such as electricity, transportation, and telecommunications.	1	35	35	-	-	3 years
14	Land Registration Database	Work with the Palestinian public sector and the private sector to ensure land ownership is effectively registered in a comprehensive database.	2	30	30	-	-	5 years
		Phase 1 Subtotal		$445	$445	-	-	
		Phase 2 Subtotal		30	30	-	-	
		Phase 3 Subtotal		-	-	-	-	
		Strategy for Reform Total (All Phases)		$475	$475	-	-	

BUILDING A FOUNDATION FOR GROWTH AND BUSINESS INVESTMENT

HUMAN CAPITAL

(US$ in mm unless otherwise specified)

#	Project	Description	Phase	Total Est. Cost	Grants	Concessional Loans	Private	Implementation Timeline
1	Career Counseling, Specialized Training, and Job Placement	Provide Palestinians—particularly youth and women—with employer-focused training, career counseling, and job placement services.	1	$10	$10	–	–	1 year; program to last 5 years
2	Technical Assistance for Creation of a Youth and Women Employment Initiative	Provide technical assistance for the Palestinian public sector to develop a comprehensive strategy to boost youth and women employment.	1	10	10	–	–	2 Years
3	Science, Technology, Engineering, and Mathematics (STEM) Commercial Partnerships	Sponsor research and development partnerships between Palestinian and international companies. Encourage international firms to partner with Palestinians in the development of new commercial technologies.	1	50	25	–	25	4 Years
4	Science, Technology, Engineering, and Mathematics (STEM) Partnerships at Research Institutions	Sponsor educational training and research and development partnerships between Palestinian and global research institutions to focus on scientific research in STEM fields.	1	50	25	–	25	4 Years
5	Technical and Vocational Training	Build the capacity of vocational institutions; work with educators to develop new curriculums to focus on high-demand areas such as healthcare, tourism, and information and communications technology (ICT); partner with the private sector to support dual vocational, work-study programs; and upgrade equipment and facilities.	1	75	40	–	35	3 years
6	Internships	Develop new internship programs for Palestinian students with subsidies for international internships.	1	50	25	–	25	1 year; program to last 10 years
7	Apprenticeships	Provide small grants to private sector companies to encourage them to develop part-time apprenticeship programs for Palestinian secondary and post-graduate school students.	1	50	10	–	40	1 year; program to last 10 years
8	In-Service Training Programs	Provide financial incentives to the private sector to expand training programs and facilities to support Palestinian employees.	1	25	25	–	–	1 year; program to last 5 years
9	Re-training Programs	Provide Palestinians in the workforce with opportunities to gain new skills and receive additional training at vocational institutions and other institutions.	1	25	25	–	–	1 year; program to last 5 years

BUILDING A FOUNDATION FOR GROWTH AND BUSINESS INVESTMENT

HUMAN CAPITAL

US$ in mm unless otherwise specified

#	Project	Description	Phase	Total Est. Cost	Grants	Concessional Loans	Private	Implementation Timeline
10	Private Sector Survey	Implement a new annual survey of private-sector companies, which will identify the demands of the labor market. The results of this survey will be shared with students, educators, and career counselors to ensure curriculum is up to date and tailored to support the needs of the private sector.	1	15	15	-	-	1 year; program to last 10 years
11	International Scholarships	Establish a scholarship program that provides Palestinian university students and graduates the opportunity to pursue degrees from top global universities. Following graduation, these students would be expected to return home, as is typical in similar programs, to become a core element of the future generation of leaders in the West Bank and Gaza.	1	300	300	-	-	1 year; program to last 6 years
12	Teacher Scholarship Program	Create an annual scholarship program benefiting Palestinian teachers, aspiring teachers, and administrators who seek to study in masters and PhD program sat top teachers colleges around the world.	1	100	100	-	-	1 year; program to last 5 years
13	Supporting Private Sector Training for Manufacturers	Support financing for large manufacturers to set up on-site training centers to grow the number of skilled workers and equip them with new skills and career opportunities, including opportunities for driving technical innovation and studying modern manufacturing processes.	1	50	50	-	-	3 years
14	Digital Economy Scholarships	Support digital economy scholarships to boost the success of Palestinian graduates in the ICT sector. University students could spend a semester at an international university program focused on the ICT sector, and graduates could spend a year at universities or companies acquiring additional skills. Recipients of the scholarship would be required to return home for a certain period of time to train and mentor high-potential Palestinian students.	1	50	50	-	-	2 years
15	Visiting Professors	Connect Palestinian teachers and professors with international academic institutions to craft reform sand new education program s. Also support visiting professors and teachers from abroad to spend a year working in Palestinian academic institutions.	2	40	40	-	-	2 years; program to last 6 years
16	Smart Schools	Provide primary, secondary, and post-secondary academic institutions with access to funding to deploy new education technology and resources.	2	100	100	-	-	5 years
17	New Palestinian University	Support the construction and development of a new flagship liberal arts and sciences university in the West Bank and Gaza.	2	500	250	250	-	5 years
			Phase 1 Subtotal	$860	$710	-	$150	
			Phase 2 Subtotal	640	390	250	-	
			Phase 3 Subtotal	-	-	-	-	
			Human Capital Total (All Phases)	$1,500	$1,100	$250	$150	

BUILDING A FOUNDATION FOR GROWTH AND BUSINESS INVESTMENT

ENTREPRENEURSHIP AND INNOVATION

US$ in mm unless otherwise is specified

#	Project	Description	Phase	Total Est. Cost	Grants	Concessional Loans	Private	Implementation Timeline
1	Seed Capital Fund / Equity Matching Capital	Support Palestinian startups with seed capital funding and equity matching to incentivize investors in Palestinian early-stage businesses.	1	$100	$100	–	–	2 Years
2	Building Innovation Centers	Work with local incubators to develop a cohesive strategy to support entrepreneurship while connecting startups with top global institutions and access to capital to support growth.	1	1C	10	–	–	2 Years
3	Startup Concessional Financing	Support the creation of lending facilities for Palestinian startups and emerging technology companies.	1	300	–	300	–	2 Years
			Phase 1 Subtotal	$410	$110	$300	–	
			Phase 2 Subtotal	–	–	–	–	
			Phase 3 Subtotal	–	–	–	–	
			Entrepreneurship and Innovation Total (All Phases)	$410	$110	$300	–	

BUILDING A FOUNDATION FOR GROWTH AND BUSINESS INVESTMENT

SMALL AND MEDIUM BUSINESSES

(US$ in mm unless otherwise specified)

#	Project	Description	Phase	Total Est. Cost	Financing Grants	Financing Concessional Loans	Financing Private	Implementation Timeline
1	Micro, Small, and Medium Enterprise (MSME) Loan Guarantee Program	Support and expand loan guarantee programs for MSMEs.	1	$40	$40	-	-	1 year
2	Micro, Small, and Medium Enterprise (MSME) Grant Facility	Provide grants for capital investments by MSMEs.	1	100	100	-	-	1 year
3	Small and Medium Business Consulting Services	In conjunction with MSME loan and grant programs, provide consulting services for Palestinian businesses as well as connections to experts and leaders in the relevant fields.	1	10	10	-	-	1 year
4	Creating Incentives for Manufacturing Investment	Support financing for new manufacturing facilities and the expansion of existing facilities.	1	100	-	100	-	3 years
5	Financial Technology (FinTech) and Low-Cost Loans for Farmers	Develop a public-private partnership to support a FinTech solution that can support farmers with financial products, such as crop insurance, micro-loans, and mobile savings accounts. This could also act as a platform to connect farmers to buyers and increase their awareness of prevailing regional and international market conditions for different crops.	1	400	30	370	-	3 years
			Phase 1 Subtotal	$650	$180	$470	-	
			Phase 2 Subtotal	-	-	-	-	
			Phase 3 Subtotal	-	-	-	-	
			Small and Medium Businesses Total (All Phases)	$650	$180	$470	-	

OPENING THE WEST BANK AND GAZA

Building new connections between Palestinians and the region will increase trade, reduce costs, and facilitate regional cooperation.

GOALS

Construct a modern West Bank – Gaza transportation network

Implement modern scanning and infrastructure solutions at key crossing points

Opening the West Bank and Gaza

Roads and Rail

Border Crossings

OPENING THE WEST BANK AND GAZA

ROADS AND RAIL

(US$ in mm unless otherwise specified)

	Project	Description	Phase	Total Est. Cost	Financing			Implementation Timeline
					Grants	Concessional Loans	Private	
1	Capacity Building: Transportation Management	Develop the capacity of Palestinian officials to manage and maintain transportation infrastructure, including crossing points. This program will also support investments in technologies that improve existing transportation infrastructure throughout the West Bank and Gaza.	1	$50	$50	–	–	2 years
2	Planning and Preparation: West Bank-Gaza Transportation Network Study	A long-term solution for an efficient connection to support the flow of goods and people between the West Bank and Gaza is essential for Palestinian and regional interconnectivity. A project of this scale will require significant planning to meet regulatory, urban planning, siting, construction, and other requirements.	1	2	2	–		2 years
3	Transportation Integration: West Bank and Gaza Road Repair	West Bank and Gaza roads are in need of immediate repair to allow for commerce and the movement of people. These projects would focus on them ost urgent and impactful road repairs.	1	200	200	–		4 years
4	Transportation Integration: West Bank and Gaza Road Improvement	Improve and expand roads and associated infrastructure, and integrate roads with upgraded crossing points.	2	200	200	–	–	7 years
5	Transportation Integration: West Bank - Gaza Transportation Network	Construct a transportation network connecting Gaza to the West Bank, which could fundamentally change the Palestinian economy. Features could include an intermodal rail line linking many of them a jor cities of Gaza and the West Bank for rapid urban transport, mass transport stations near urban centers, and connections to regional railways such as the Jordan railway project. This connection will occur in stages, with an interim solution planned for implementation within two years.	3	5,030	–	3,750	1,250	8 years
6	Transportation Integration: West Bank and Gaza New Road Construction	Construct new roads throughout the West Bank and Gaza to ensure the efficient and secure flow of goods and people.	3	200	200	–	–	7 years
		Phase 1 Subtotal		$252	$252	–	–	
		Phase 2 Subtotal		200	200	–	–	
		Phase 3 Subtotal		5,200	200	3,750	1,250	
		Roads and Rail Total (All Phases)		$5,652	$652	$3,750	$1,250	

OPENING THE WEST BANK AND GAZA

BORDER CROSSINGS

(US$ in millions unless otherwise specified)

	Project	Description	Phase	Total Est. Cost	Financing Grants	Concessional Loans	Private	Implementation Timeline
1	Technical Support for Crossing Point Management	Develop the capacity of Palestinian officials to manage crossing points while adhering to international security standards and best practices, with an emphasis on anti-corruption safeguards.	1	$10	$10	--	--	1 Year
2	Upgraded Crossing Points – Stage 1	Develop the essential infrastructure necessary to reduce the costs of trade and sustain economic development in the West Bank and Gaza, including upgraded scanners and new technological solutions to support rapid and secure transit of goods and people. Expand roads at key crossing points, including the Allenby crossing between the West Bank and Jordan, and examine the creation of new crossing points to create additional trade capacity. In the short term, funding could be provided to support increased staffing and hours of operation.	1	250	250	--	--	4 years
3	Upgraded Crossing Points – Stage 2	Upgrade crossing points to include additional technological solutions and to support the efficient and secure flow of material and finished goods.	2	300	300	--	--	6 years
4	Upgraded Crossing Points – Stage 3	Ensure that all critical crossing points are constructed to satisfy the long-term commercial and transit requirements of the Palestinians.	3	350	350	--	--	10 years
		Phase 1 Subtotal		$260	$260	--	--	
		Phase 2 Subtotal		300	300	--	--	
		Phase 3 Subtotal		350	350	--	--	
		Border Crossings Total (All Phases)		$910	$910	--	--	

CONSTRUCTING ESSENTIAL INFRASTRUCTURE

Investing in more electricity, cleaner water, and transformative digital services.

GOALS

Ensure continual availability of affordable electricity in the West Bank and Gaza

Double the potable water supply per capita available to the Palestinians

Enable Palestinian high-speed data services

Constructing
Essential
Infrastructure

Power

Water and Wastewater

Digital Services

POWER

US$ in mm unless otherwise specified)

#	Project	Description	Phase	Total Est. Cost	Financing			Implementation Timeline
					Grants	Concessional Loans	Private	
1	Fuel Supply: Diesel Fuel Storage Tanks for Gaza Power Plant	Rebuild storage tanks to support the operational stability of the Gaza Power Plant.	1	$5	$5	-	-	6 months
2	Power Generation: Generators for Gaza short-term power	Provide large-scale generators and fuel supply for an immediate power solution for primary health care centers, water and sanitation utilities, municipal buildings, and other critical users.	1	10	10	-	-	1 Year
3	Cross Border Services: Repair Egypt-Gaza Transmission Lines	Rehabilitate existing Egyptian lines connected to Gaza.	1	12	12	-	-	1 Year
4	Power Generation: Solar Energy System - Stage 1 (100 MW for Gaza)	Develop new Gaza solar facilities, including rooftop and larger solar arrays.	1	150	-	113	38	3 Years
5	Transmission: Short-term Transmission & Distribution Repair	Rapid rehabilitation, improvement, and expansion of the transmission and distribution grid in Gaza and the West Bank.	1	20	20	-	-	2 years
6	Revenue Collection: Prepaid Meters	Install prepaid meters in low-collection areas to increase revenues.	1	40	40	-	-	2 years
7	Electricity Resiliency for Essential Services: Micro-Grid Systems for Hospitals and Schools - Stage 1	Utilize micro-grid systems that have the ability to operate independently or as part of the grid. These packages of solar, storage, and fossil energy would provide resiliency and reliability for hospitals, primary and secondary schools, universities, and industrial and manufacturing centers.	1	50	-	38	13	4 years

POWER

US$ in m unless otherwise specified

#	Project	Description	Phase	Total Est. Cost	Financing Grants	Financing Concessional Loans	Financing Private	Implementation Timeline
8	Capacity Building: Technical Assistance and Training - Stage 1	Provide technical assistance to Palestinian institutions to build capacity for grid management and maintenance; tariff determination, implementation, and collection; and system upgrades. "SmartGrid" solutions in both the West Bank and Gaza could improve efficiency by lowering losses, non-collections, and overhead costs. By using digital and other advanced technologies to monitor and manage the transport and distribution of electricity, smart grids would increase system reliability, resilience, and stability while decreasing the cost of technical and commercial losses.	1	10	10	–	–	Years 1-2 of program
9	Cross Border Services: Upgrade Egypt-Gaza Transmission Lines - Stage 1	Increase the power supply from Egypt to Gaza by upgrading transmission lines to support a total capacity of 50MW.	1	10	10	–	–	1 year
10	Cross Border Services: Upgrade Egypt-Gaza Lines - Stage 2	Increase the power supply from Egypt to Gaza by upgrading transmission lines to support a total capacity of 100MW.	1	20	20	–	–	3 years
11	Transmission: Israel-Gaza 161 Kv Line	Construct a high voltage 161 kV line from the Israeli electricity grid to Gaza.	1	44	44	–	–	3 years
12	Fuel Supply: Natural Gas Pipeline to Gaza Power Plant (Gas for Gaza)	Construct a natural gas pipeline connecting Gaza to the Israeli natural gas network. This pipeline could receive natural gas from the Israeli network or, in the future, from the Gaza Marine natural gas field. This project will support the conversion of the Gaza Power Plant from diesel fuel to natural gas.	1	80	20	45	15	3 years
13	Power Generation: Gaza Power Plant Natural Gas Conversion and Upgrade - Stage 1	Convert the Gaza Power Plant (GPP) from diesel fuel to natural gas. This includes replacing diesel-running units with dual-running units (diesel and gas), modifying the control system, and constructing a gas pressure control unit.	1	10	–	8	3	3 years
14	Power Generation: Solar Energy System Stage 2 (100 MW for West Bank)	Implement Stage 2 of solar energy projects for the West Bank, including utility scale and larger industrial projects.	2	150	–	113	38	5 years
15	Transmission: West Bank and Gaza Transmission & Distribution System Upgrade	Rehabilitate, improve, and expand the transmission and distribution grid in Gaza and the West Bank. Construct five new high-voltage substations in the West Bank to support additional electricity imports from Israel.	2	150	38	113	–	5 years

POWER

US$ in mm unless otherwise specified)

#	Project	Description	Total Est. Phase	Cost	Financing Grants	Concessional Loans	Private	Implementation Timeline
16	Electricity Resiliency for Key Businesses: Micro-Grid Systems for Industrial and Manufacturing - Stage 2	Implement Stage 2 of the micro-grid system sproject with a focus on industrial land manufacturing custom ers and other critical institutions.	2	100	-	75	25	5 years
17	Capacity Building: Technical Assistance and Training - Stage 2	Implement Stage 2 of the technical assistance and training program to train utility officials, implementa sustainable payment collection system, and build capacity to m anage and m aintain the electric grid.	2	10	10	-	-	Years 3-5 of program
18	Power Generation: Gaza Power Plant Natural Gas Conversion and Upgrade - Stage 2	Expand the Gaza Power Plant by constructing additional natural gas turbines.	3	500	-	375	125	6-8 years
19	Power Generation: Jenin Power Plant	Construct a gas-fired power plant in Jenin to provide electricity in the northern West Bank.	3	600	-	450	150	8 years
20	Power Generation: Hebron Power Plant	Construct a gas-fired power plant in Hebron to provide electricity in the southern West Bank.	3	600	-	450	150	10 years
21	Capacity Building: Technical Assistance and Training - Stage 3	Implement Stage 3 of the technical assistance and training program to support additional capacity and technical requirements as the Palestinian power system grows in size and complexity.	3	10	10	-	-	Years 6-10 of program
			Phase 1 Subtotal	$461	$191	$203	$68	
			Phase 2 Subtotal	410	48	300	63	
			Phase 3 Subtotal	1,710	10	1,275	425	
			Power Total (All Phases)	$2,581	$249	$1,778	$555	

CONSTRUCTING ESSENTIAL INFRASTRUCTURE

WATER AND WASTEWATER

(US$ in mm unless otherwise specified)

#	Project	Description	Phase	Total Est. Cost	Financing — Grants	Concessional Loans	Private	Implementation Timeline
1	Water Supply: Imports from Israel	Provide immediately impactful solutions to potable water needs in Gaza and the West Bank by increasing imports from Israel.	1	$50	$25	$25	–	Immediate
2	Water Supply: Short-term low-volume (STLV) desalination plants	Construct 10 new STLV desalination plants in Gaza to provide quick access to potable water.	1	100	100	–	–	2 years
3	Water Treatment: North Gaza Emergency Sewage Treatment (NGEST) Project Support	Fund the non-revenue water reduction plan, support operations and maintenance costs, and add additional solar power capacity for NGEST.	1	20	20	–	–	2 years
4	Water Treatment: Khan Younis Wastewater Treatment Plant	Add solar power capacity and support operations and maintenance costs at the Khan Younis Wastewater Treatment Plant.	1	20	20	–	–	2 years
5	Water Delivery: Grid Package - Stage 1	Implement a package of priority water infrastructure projects to support an expanded water grid and to increase efficiency.	1	50	25	25	–	3 years
6	Water Treatment: North Gaza Emergency Sewage Treatment (NGEST) Project Expansion	Expand the NGEST plant and implement a re-use scheme.	2	40	25	15	–	5 years
7	Water Treatment: Wastewater Infrastructure Package	Implement a package of priority wastewater treatment and wastewater re-use infrastructure projects.	2	350	175	131	44	5 years
8	Water Delivery: Grid Package - Stage 2	Continue to develop necessary water infrastructure through priority projects for water network integration.	2	67	33	33	–	5 years

WATER AND WASTEWATER

US$ in mm unless otherwise specified

	Project	Description	Phase	Total Est. Cost	Financing Grants	Concessional Loans	Private	Implementation Timeline
9	Water Supply: Gaza Central Desalination Plant (GCDP) and Associated Works	Support the main components of the GCDP program, including the desalination facility, the North-South carrier, and other network improvements. Also support in plan implementation of the non-revenue water reduction plan to ensure the financial sustainability of the sector.	2	125	125	–	–	5 years
10	Water Delivery: West Bank Distribution Network Extension & Rehabilitation	Build new connections; implementa in a pipe network extension and rehabilitation; and construct new storage tanks.	2	500	375	125	–	5 years
11	Water Supply: West Bank Wells	Construct and repair existing wells to increase the amount of groundwater available.	2	140	88	52	–	5 years
12	Water Supply: Reservoirs and Rainwater Capture Projects	Support the necessary infrastructure to increase the amount of harvested rainwater from 6 million cubic meters / year to 25 million cubic meters / year.	2	30	30	–	–	5 years
13	Water Supply: Gaza Central Desalination Plant (GCDP) Expansion	Expand the existing desalination facility to increase its capacity and expand the plant's energy capacity.	3	180	90	90	–	6 years
14	Water Delivery: Wastewater Infrastructure Package Extension	Complete the build-out of wastewater infrastructure with long-term projects for treatment capacity, the sewage network, and critical connections.	3	600	300	225	75	8-10 years
15	Water Delivery: Grid Package - Stage 3	Continue to upgrade connections to the smart water grid system for industry, business, agriculture, hospitals, residential, and public infrastructure.	3	50	31	19	–	8-10 years
		Phase 1 Subtotal		$240	$190	$50	–	
		Phase 2 Subtotal		1,252	851	357	44	
		Phase 3 Subtotal		830	421	334	75	
		Water and Wastewater Total (All Phases)		$2,322	$1,462	$741	$119	

DIGITAL SERVICES

US$ in mm unless otherwise specified

#	Project	Description	Phase	Total Est. Cost	Financing Grants	Concessional Loans	Private	Implementation Timeline
1	Improving Technology: Palestinian Internet Infrastructure - Stage 1	Upgrade Palestinian internet capabilities, particularly related to mobile data services. In coordination with the relevant authorities, this initiative would take a phased approach to lay the groundwork for the introduction of advanced spectrum services (5G) for the West Bank and Gaza. The program would also support high-speed broadband and WiFi capabilities. These capabilities would support related economic activity in fields like software development and telecom services.	1	$250	-	$125	$125	4 years
2	Human Capital: Digital Economy Scholarships - Stage 1	Support digital economy scholarships to boost the success of Palestinian graduates in the ICT sector. University students could spend a semester at an international university program focused on the ICT sector, and graduates could spend a year at universities or companies acquiring additional skills. Recipients of the scholarship would be required to return home for a certain period of time to train and mentor high potential Palestinian students.	1	10	10	-	-	1 year
3	Improving Technology: Palestinian Internet Infrastructure - Stage 2	Expand the Palestinian internet infrastructure and support capacity building and technical assistance for maintenance and robust private-sector competition. Construct an antenna in kiosks in the West Bank and Gaza that provide high-speed WiFi, device charging, access to city services, maps, and directions.	2	325	-	244	81	6 years
4	Human Capital: Digital Economy Scholarships - Stage 2	Extend the Digital Economy Scholarships program.	2	15	15	-	-	3 Years
5	Improving Technology: Palestinian Internet Infrastructure - Stage 3	Expand Palestinian internet infrastructure, including the deployment of infrastructure to support 5G services.	3	2,000	-	1,500	500	5-7 years
6	Human Capital: Digital Economy Scholarships - Stage 3	Extend the Digital Economy Scholarships program.	3	25	25	-	-	6 years
			Phase 1 Subtotal	$260	$10	$125	$125	
			Phase 2 Subtotal	340	15	244	81	
			Phase 3 Subtotal	2,025	25	1,500	500	
			Digital Services Total (All Phases)	$2,625	$50	$1,869	$706	

PROMOTING PRIVATE-SECTOR GROWTH

Injecting capital into strategic sectors will generate high-quality jobs and open up opportunities for upward and mobility.

GOALS

Increase foreign direct investment as a component of Palestinian GDP from 1.4 percent to 8 percent

Promoting Private-Sector Growth

Tourism

Agriculture

Housing

Manufacturing

Natural Resources

TOURISM

(US$ in mm unless otherwise specified)

	Project	Description	Phase	Total Est. Cost	Financing Grants	Financing Concessional Loans	Financing Private	Implementation Timeline
1	Restoration and Development: Tourism Sites and Accommodations - Stage 1	Quickly implement repairs and the restoration of historical and religious sites as well as beachfront areas, and provide assistance for hotel and tour operators to quickly increase capacity and improve existing facilities.	1	$100	$50	$40	$10	2 years
2	Marketing: Global Tourism Campaign	Support a global marketing campaign to emphasize the significance of historical and religious sites and promote Palestinian culture.	1	50	50	–	–	2 years
3	Capacity Building: Hospitality Education Hub	Support the creation of a hospitality education hub in the West Bank and Gaza, which could look in partnership with leading international hospitality schools—such as the United Arab Emirates Academy of Hospitality—to provide best-in-class education for students to improve the quality of service at tourist sites. The hospitality hub could provide academic cooperation, academic exchange programs, and joint projects with international hospitality schools.	1	50	50	–	–	3 years
4	Restoration and Development: Tourism Sites and Accommodations - Stage 2	Repair, restore, and upgrade historical and religious sites, beachfront areas, and urban centers to support increased tourism. Support the development and the preservation of existing archeological sites.	2	250	150	75	25	6 years
5	Construction: West Bank and Gaza Hotels/Resorts - Stage 1	Construct additional hotels close to popular tourist sites.	2	500	–	375	125	5 years
6	Construction: West Bank and Gaza Hotels/Resorts - Stage 2	Grow the tourism industry through the support of additional private-sector investments in the West Bank and Gaza.	3	500	–	375	125	10 years
			Phase 1 Subtotal	$200	$150	$40	$10	
			Phase 2 Subtotal	750	150	450	150	
			Phase 3 Subtotal	500	–	375	125	
			Tourism Total (All Phases)	$1,450	$300	$865	$285	

PROMOTING PRIVATE-SECTOR GROWTH

AGRICULTURE

US$ in mm unless otherwise specified)

	Project	Description	Phase	Total Est. Cost	Financing Grants	Concessional Loans	Private	Implementation Timeline
1	Access To Finance: Financial Technology (FinTech) and Low Cost Loans for Farmers	Develop a public-private partnership to support a FinTech solution that can support farmers with financial products, such as crop insurance, micro-loans, and mobile savings accounts. This could also act as a platform to connect farmers to buyers and increase their awareness of prevailing regional and international market conditions for different crops.	1	$400	$30	$370	-	3 years
2	Supply Chain Infrastructure: Cold Storage	Develop cold storage facilities and trucks at key points—including crossing points—to reduce spoilage.	1	60	60	-	-	3 years
3	Supply Chain Infrastructure: Packaging and processing	Provide support to food processing and packaging facilities to expand operations.	2	75	-	75	-	5 years
4	Irrigation: West Bank Irrigation Initiative	Increase irrigation in the West Bank and Gaza to boost yields and increase the capacity of farmers to grow high-value crops.	2	200	-	150	50	5 years
5	Capacity Building: Center for Agricultural Innovation	Establish a center to provide farmers with access to trained technical specialists, new technology, and a connection to businesses across the value chain. This center could work with farmers to apply best practices in areas including precision irrigation systems, greenhouses, and the cultivation of new cash crops, as well as provide grants and other financial support to farmers seeking to apply new technologies and techniques.	3	25	25	-	-	8 years
6	Restoration and Development: Land Rehabilitation	Cultivate land—particularly in the West Bank—for agricultural use to increase Palestinian agricultural output.	3	150	-	113	38	8 years
		Phase 1 Subtotal		$460	$90	$370	-	
		Phase 2 Subtotal		275	-	225	50	
		Phase 3 Subtotal		175	25	113	38	
		Agriculture Total (All Phases)		$910	$115	$708	$88	

HOUSING

US$ in mm unless otherwise specified

	Project	Description	Phase	Total Est. Cost	Financing			Implementation Timeline
					Grants	Concessional Loans	Private	
1	Access to Finance: Mortgage Facility and Home Ownership Subsidies - Stage 1	Create a mortgage-lending facility to support Palestinian borrowers and jumpstart the Palestinian mortgage market. This facility would aim to decrease the housing affordability gap for new buyers by providing a new long-term financing option.	1	$400	$200	$200	–	3 years
2	Access to Finance: Mortgage Facility and Home Ownership Subsidies - Stage 2	Extend Stage 1 of program.	2	600	300	300	–	7 years
			Phase 1 Subtotal	$400	$200	$200	–	
			Phase 2 Subtotal	600	300	300	–	
			Phase 3 Subtotal	–	–	–	–	
			Housing Total (All Phases)	$1,000	$500	$500	–	

PROMOTING PRIVATE-SECTOR GROWTH

MANUFACTURING

(US$ in mm unless otherwise specified)

#	Project	Description	Phase	Total Est. Cost	Financing Grants	Financing Concessional Loans	Financing Private	Implementation Timeline
1	Supply Chain Infrastructure: Bonded Warehouse – Project 1	Support a jointly-established bonded warehouse within investments in special economic zones to reduce transaction costs and facilitate trade. A bonded warehouse would be subject to a bilateral operating agreement and can complement the established transit facilities between Israel and the West Bank and Gaza. These facilities would be built to integrate with the envisioned technological upgrades at crossing points.	1	$25	$25	-	-	3 years
2	Incentivizing Investment: Industrial Park – Project 1	Develop a joint industrial park along the border areas, supported by financial incentives and political risk insurance to attract foreign direct investment.	1	50	50	-	-	3 years
3	Supply Chain Infrastructure: Investing in Modern Trucking Fleet	Support financing for a new fleet of trucks for ease of loading and shipment tagging.	1	50	-	50	-	3 years
4	Access to Finance: Creating Incentives for Investment	Support financing for new manufacturing facilities and the expansion of existing facilities.	1	100	-	100	-	3 years
5	Human Capital: Supporting Private Sector Training	Support financing for large manufacturers to set up on-site training centers to grow the number of skilled workers and equip them with new skills and career opportunities, including opportunities for driving technical innovation and studying modern manufacturing processes.	1	50	50	-	-	3 years
6	Supply Chain Infrastructure: Bonded Warehouse – Project 2	Support a second joint bonded warehouse project at greater scale.	2	50	-	38	13	5 years
7	Incentivizing Investment: Industrial Park – Project 2	Support additional industrial park projects along the border area.	2	100	-	75	25	5 years
8	Raw Materials Production: Cement Factory	Support a cement factory in the West Bank for the Palestinian construction industry.	2	300	-	225	75	5 years
9	Supply Chain Infrastructure: Bonded Warehouse – Project 3	Support a third large-scale joint bonded warehouse.	3	50	-	38	13	6 years
10	Incentivizing Investment: Industrial Park – Project 3	Support additional large-scale industrial park projects.	3	100	-	75	25	6 years
			Phase 1 Subtotal	$275	$125	$150	-	
			Phase 2 Subtotal	450	-	338	113	
			Phase 3 Subtotal	150	-	113	38	
			Manufacturing Total (All Phases)	$875	$125	$600	$150	

NATURAL RESOURCES

US$ in mm unless otherwise specified)

#	Project	Description	Phase	Total Est. Cost	Grants	Concessional Loans	Private	Implementation Timeline
1	Gaza Marine	Support the development of the Gaza Marine gas field. Estimated to hold 1.5 trillion cubic feet (tcf) of natural gas, Gaza Marine is a potential gas source for Gaza, which could provide the independent capability to fuel the Gaza Power Plant and the local Gaza economy.	2	$1,000	-	$750	$250	8 years
2	Quarrying Industry Support	Support the development of an expanded Palestinian quarrying industry.	2	50	-	38	13	5 Years
3	Technical Assistance for Natural Resource Extraction	Provide technical assistance for Palestinian natural resources companies to build expertise in modern extraction practices.	2	10	10	-	-	5 Years
4	Oil and Gas Exploration and Production	Explore oil and gas exploration and production in the West Bank and Gaza to the extent agreed by the parties on resource rights.	3	390	-	293	98	8 years
		Phase 1 Subtotal		-	-	-	-	
		Phase 2 Subtotal		1,050	10	788	263	
		Phase 3 Subtotal		390	-	293	98	
		Natural Resources Total (All Phases)		$1,450	$10	$1,080	$360	

Financing

STRENGTHENING REGIONAL DEVELOPMENT AND INTEGRATION

Creating new opportunities for Palestinian businesses and increasing commerce with neighboring countries.

GOALS

Increase Palestinian exports as a percentage of GDP from 17 to 40

Strengthening Regional Devebpm ent and Integration

Jordan

Egypt

Lebanon

STRENGTHENING REGIONAL DEVELOPMENT AND INTEGRATION

JORDAN

(US$ in mm unless otherwise specified)

#	Project	Description	Phase	Total Est. Cost	Financing Concessional Grants	Loans	Private	Implementation Timeline
1	Regional Trade and Commerce: Allenby, Amman, Zarqa Bus Rapid Transit	Support a new bus system that would connect the cities of Amman and Zarqa, Jordan's two largest cities, as well as points within each city.	1	$150	$150	-	-	4 years
2	Cross Border Services: Red Sea-Dead Sea Conveyance – Stage 1	Provide support for the "Red-Dead" project, which will provide water to Israel and Jordan while also slowing the declining water levels in the Dead Sea. Key features are envisioned to include a desalination plant on the Red Sea to provide water to southern areas of Jordan and Israel, the sale of Israeli water to northern Jordan, an Israeli-Palestinian agreement for provision of the additional water to the West Bank and Gaza, and brine production from the Red Sea desalination plant to be combined with sea water and sent to the Dead Sea to reverse declining water levels.	1	145	145	-	-	2 years
3	Economic Stabilization: Solar Program	Support the continued development of Jordan's solar power generation program.	1	150	-	75	75	3 years
4	Economic Stabilization: Jordan SME Fund	Expand the existing U.S. Overseas Private Investment Corporation (OPIC) program, which supports small and medium enterprises (SMEs) in the region. OPIC could create an expanded guarantee facility for loans to SMEs in Jordan.	1	125	-	125	-	2 years
5	Economic Stabilization: National Broadband Network	Install a broadband, fiber-optic network in Jordan to connect public schools, hospitals and healthcare centers, businesses, and government entities in areas including, but not limited to, Irbid, Mafraq, Jerash and Ajloun.	1	100	100	-	-	3 years
6	Economic Stabilization: National Data Center	Create a central office, under the National Information Technology Center, with technical infrastructure and equipment to house all of the Jordanian government's electronic data.	1	70	70	-	-	2 years

STRENGTHENING REGIONAL DEVELOPMENT AND INTEGRATION

JORDAN

US$ in mm unless otherwise specified

#	Project	Description	Phase	Total Est. Cost	Grants	Concessional Loans	Private	Implementation Timeline
						Financing		
7	Regional Trade and Commerce: Develop and Upgrade Airports	Improve facilities at King Hussein and Marka Airports and develop a new airport in southern Shuna.	2	650	–	325	325	6 years
8	Cross Border Services: Red Sea-Dead Sea Conveyance - Stage 2	Support continued development onto the Red Sea-Dead Sea conveyance project.	2	400	400	–	–	6 years
9	Cross Border Services: Jordan River Improvement Project	Implement a mitigation program to rehabilitate the Jordan River and prevent pollution from agricultural land w as few a term run-offs.	2	250	250	–	–	6 years
10	Economic Stabilization: National Cybersecurity Infrastructure and Capacity Building	Build a national cybersecurity capability and provide technical assistance to support Jordanian efforts to protect both public and private sectors, including banks, hospitals, and critical infrastructure, against state and non-state cyber attackers, as well as open up opportunities for more international cyber collaboration.	2	500	500	–	–	5 years
11	Market Integration: Ma'an Dry Port	Establish a dry port in Ma'an that will serve the industrial park in Ma'an governorate, close to the proposed route of the national rail way project, and connect it to several national land international land roads with neighboring countries and key trade infrastructure.	2	50	50	–	–	5 years
12	Regional Trade and Commerce: Jordan + Regional Rail Network	Support Jordan's proposed national railroad project to develop a regional rail network connecting Amman to Aqaba, which would decrease the cost of shipments and trade from Jordan's main population centers, and a potential additional rail extension to the Arabian Gulf.	3	1,825	–	913	913	10 years
13	Regional Trade and Commerce: Jordan Transport Corridors	Improve Jordan's road infrastructure including the four primary corridors, two of which are primarily for regional trade and can support increased trade with the West Bank and Gaza. These improvements will help enhance road safety and reduce the cost of transportation and trade.	3	1,530	–	750	750	10 years
14	Cross Border Services: Jordan—West Bank Transmission Line	Upgrade the Jordan-West Bank interconnection by building a 400 kV line.	3	50	38	13	–	10 years
15	Regional Tourism: Aqaba's Corniche District / High Lakes Resort	Support the creation of a resort built on land north of Aqaba's coast and adjacent to the Marsa Zayed project, as well as the development onto Aqaba's Corniche District including waterparks, an ecological park, beaches, and hotels. These development will boost interregional tourism packages, which will also support the tourism industry of the West Bank and Gaza.	3	1,400	–	700	700	10 years
	Jordan Phase 1 Subtotal			$740	$465	$200	$75	
	Jordan Phase 2 Subtotal			1,850	1,200	325	325	
	Jordan Phase 3 Subtotal			4,775	38	2,375	2,363	
	Jordan Total (All Phases)			$7,365	$1,703	$2,900	$2,763	

STRENGTHENING REGIONAL DEVELOPMENT AND INTEGRATION

EGYPT

US$ in mm unless otherwise specified

	Project	Description	Phase	Total Est. Cost	Financing Grants	Concessional Loans	Private	Implementation Timeline
1	Economic Stabilization: Egypt SME Fund	Expand the existing U.S. Overseas Private Investment Corporation (OPIC) program, which supports small and medium enterprises (SMEs) in the region. OPIC could create an expanded guarantee facility for loans to SMEs in Egypt.	1	$125	-	$125	-	2 years
2	Cross Border Services: Repair Egypt-Gaza Transmission Lines	Rehabilitate existing Egyptian lines connected to Gaza. Palestinians would then be able to purchase additional power from Egypt at an agreed price to be negotiated by the parties.	1	12	12	-	-	1 Year
3	Cross Border Services: Upgrade Egypt-Gaza Transmission Lines - Stage 1	Increase power supply from Egypt to Gaza by upgrading transmission lines to support a total capacity of 50MW. Palestinians would then be able to purchase additional power from Egypt at an agreed price to be negotiated by the parties.	1	10	10	-	-	1 year
4	Cross Border Services: Upgrade Egypt-Gaza Lines - Stage 2	Increase power supply from Egypt to Gaza by upgrading transmission lines to support a total capacity of 100MW. Palestinians would then be able to purchase additional power from Egypt at an agreed price to be negotiated by the parties.	1	20	20	-	-	3 years
5	Regional Trade and Commerce: Qualifying Industrial Zones	Explore ways to better utilize Egyptian Qualifying Industrial Zones (QIZs) to promote increased trade between Egypt, Israel, and the West Bank and Gaza. Key features of this program could include review of potential adjustments to the share of Egyptian, Israeli, or Palestinian content required to meet the 35 percent content requirement.	1	-	-	-	-	2 years
6	Regional Trade and Commerce: Eastern Mediterranean Energy Hub	Support the establishment of a regional natural gas hub in Egypt to benefit from the growing offshore natural gas production in the Eastern Mediterranean. This project could increase exports to international markets from Egyptian LNG terminals, as well as increase supply for the Egyptian domestic market. A natural gas hub in Egypt would help coordinate energy development in the Eastern Mediterranean.	2	1,500	-	450	1,050	5 years
7	Regional Trade and Commerce: Suez Canal Economic Zone	Support port expansions and business incentives for the Egyptian trade hub near the Suez Canal.	2	500	250	250	-	5 years

STRENGTHENING REGIONAL DEVELOPMENT AND INTEGRATION

EGYPT

US$ in mm unless otherwise specified)

Project	Description	Phase	Total Est. Cost	Financing Grants	Financing Concessional Loans	Financing Private	Implementation Timeline
8 Economic Stabilization: Sinai Power Development	Support power generation projects in the Sinai to increase the supply for new developments.	2	500	125	250	125	5 years
9 Economic Stabilization: Sinai Water Development	Support water infrastructure projects in the Sinai to bolster broader economic development.	2	500	125	250	125	5 years
10 Regional Trade and Commerce: Sinai Transportation	Support Sinai roads and transport infrastructure to connect new developments.	2	500	250	250	-	5 years
11 Economic Stabilization: Sinai Tourism Development	Support Sinai tourism projects including along the Red Sea coast.	3	500	125	250	125	8 years
12 Regional Trade and Commerce: Transport and Logistics Modernization Program	Support new transportation infrastructure in Egypt to improve domestic and regional connectivity.	3	5,000	-	2,500	2,500	10 years
Egypt Phase 1 Subtotal			$157	$42	$125	-	
Egypt Phase 2 Subtotal			3,500	750	1,450	1,300	
Egypt Phase 3 Subtotal			5,500	125	2,750	2,625	
Egypt Total (All Phases)			$9,167	$917	$4,325	$3,925	

STRENGTHENING REGIONAL DEVELOPMENT AND INTEGRATION

LEBANON

(US$ in mm unless otherwise specified)

	Project	Description	Phase	Total Est. Cost	Financing			Implementation Timeline
					Grants	Concessional Loans	Private	
1	Regional Trade and Commerce: Building Intra-regional Trade and Investments in Lebanon	Support regional trade integration to incentivize exporters to become engaged in regional value chains to significantly reduce the cost of doing business in the region.	1	$200	$200	-	-	4 years
2	Economic Stabilization: Lebanon SME Fund	Expand the existing U.S. Overseas Private Investment Corporation (OPIC) program, which supports small and medium enterprises (SMEs) in the region. OPIC could create an expanded guarantee facility for loans to SMEs in Lebanon.	1	125	-	125	-	4 years
3	Regional Trade and Commerce: Lebanon Economic Corridor & Regional Integration Program - Roads	Repair and improve Lebanese road corridors, including missing highway links primarily on the two main corridors (North-South, and East-West), which are part of the regional highway network.	3	3,000	-	2,250	750	6 years
4	Regional Trade and Commerce: Lebanon Economic Corridor & Regional Integration Program - Rail	Support the construction of a railway network within Lebanon with the potential to connect to a regional railway network.	3	2,000	250	1,500	250	8 years
5	Regional Trade and Commerce: Lebanon Economic Corridor & Regional Integration Program - Air/Sea	Support the construction and associated logistics for the expansion of the Beirut airport and other airports, the expansion of Lebanese ports including Beirut and Tripoli, and the modernization of border crossings.	3	1,000	-	750	250	8 years
		Lebanon Phase 1 Subtotal		$325	$200	$125	-	
		Lebanon Phase 2 Subtotal		-	-	-	-	
		Lebanon Phase 3 Subtotal		6,000	250	4,500	1,250	
		Lebanon Total (All Phases)		$6,325	$450	$4,625	$1,250	

EMPOWERING THE PALESTINIAN PEOPLE

Accountable
& Agile
Government

Empowered
& Prosperous
People

Thriving
& Integrated
Economy

2

EMPOWERING
THE
PALESTINIAN
PEOPLE

Enhancing
Education
Services

Strengthening
Workforce
Development

Investing in
Healthcare

Improving
Quality of Life

ENHANCING EDUCATION SERVICES

Transforming existing institutions, creating incentives for curriculum reform, supporting training for teachers, and building new partnerships with universities around the world.

GOALS

Boost human capital development in the West Bank and Gaza, achieving a 0.70 score on World Bank Human Capital Index

Establish at least one Palestinian university in the global top 150

Revise educational training, with attention to matching private-sector needs

Enhancing Education Services

Educational Quality

Educational Access

Educational Affordability

ENHANCING EDUCATION SERVICES

EDUCATIONAL QUALITY

US$ in mm unless otherwise specified

#	Project	Description	Total Phase	Total Est. Cost	Financing Grants	Concessional Loans	Private	Implementation Timeline
1	Local Certification Program	Provide educators with the opportunity to receive in-service teacher qualification certification, and principal certification while revamping pre-service teacher option program s.!	1	$40	$40	–	–	2 years
2	Incentivizing Academic Excellence	Invest in a new program to provide financial incentives to academic institutions and local governments for meeting certain benchmarks of academic excellence, including in proving curriculums, standards, post-graduation employment statistics, and education in language and soft skills such as team work, leadership, motivation, and civic engagement.	1	400	400	–	–	2 years; program to last 5 years
3	Administrator Exchanges	Develop partnerships and exchanges between local and top-ranked global academic institutions. Administrators from these institutions will engage in exchanges to discuss best practices.	1	20	20	–	–	2 years; program to last 6 years
4	Private Sector Survey	Implement a new annual survey of private-sector companies, which will identify the demands of the labor market. The results of this survey will be shared with students, educators, and career counselors to ensure curriculum stays up to date and tailored to support the needs of the private sector.	1	15	15	–	–	1 year; program to last 10 years
5	Annual Evaluations	Support the development of new approaches to evaluating student and teacher performance based on uniform quality and competency-based metrics. These reviews will be provided to administrators, teachers, and parents to ensure that students' needs are being met.	1	30	30	–	–	2 years; program to last 10 years
6	Visiting Professors	Connect Palestinian teachers and professors with international academic institutions to experience new education program s. Also support visiting professors and teachers from abroad to spend a year working in Palestinian academic institutions.	2	40	40	–	–	2 years; program to last 6 years
7	Smart Schools	Provide primary, secondary, and post-secondary academic institutions with access to funding to deploy new education technology and resources.	2	100	100	–	–	5 years
		Phase 1 Subtotal		$505	$505	–	–	
		Phase 2 Subtotal		140	140	–	–	
		Phase 3 Subtotal		–	–	–	–	
		Educational Quality Total (All Phases)		$645	$645	–	–	

ENHANCING EDUCATION SERVICES

EDUCATIONAL ACCESS

US$ in mm unless otherwise specified

	Project	Description	Total		Financing			Implementation Timeline
			Phase	Est. Cost	Grants	Concessional Loans	Private	
1	After-School Programs	Support new after-school programs and NGOs that provide primary and secondary school students with opportunities to pursue activities and develop new skills in music, sports, vocational activities, and community development.	1	$50	$50	-	-	1 year; program to last ten years
2	Constructing New Primary and Secondary Schools	Construct new schools in underserved areas to keep pace with population growth and ensure all Palestinians have access to an affordable, quality education. This program will also help streamline the regulatory process for opening a new school.	2	100	100	-	-	5 years
3	Early Childhood Education Program	Provide incentives to Palestinian public schools and private education providers to improve the quality and accessibility of early childhood education, including by expanding the number of classrooms and working to improve teaching methods.	2	200	200	-	-	5 years
4	New Palestinian University	Support the construction and development of a new flagship liberal arts and sciences university in the West Bank and Gaza.	2	500	250	250	-	5 years
		Phase 1 Subtotal		$50	$50	-	-	
		Phase 2 Subtotal		800	550	250	-	
		Phase 3 Subtotal		-	-	-	-	
		Educational Access Total (All Phases)		$850	$600	$250	-	

ENHANCING EDUCATION SERVICES

EDUCATIONAL AFFORDABILITY

US$ in mm unless otherwise specified

	Project	Description	Total			Financing			Implementation Timeline
			Phase	Est. Cost	Grants	Concessional Loans	Private		
1	International Scholarships	Establish a scholarship program that provides Palestinian university students and graduates the opportunity to pursue degrees from top global universities. Following graduation, these students would be expected to return home, as is typical in countries with similar programs, to become a core element of the future generation of leaders in the West Bank and Gaza.	1	$300	$300	–	–		1 year; program to last 6 years
2	Teacher Scholarship Program	Create an annual scholarship program benefiting Palestinian teachers, aspiring teachers, and administrators who seek to study in masters and PhD programs at top teachers colleges around the world.	1	100	100	–	–		1 year; program to last 5 years
		Phase 1 Subtotal		$400	$400	–	–		
		Phase 2 Subtotal		–	–	–	–		
		Phase 3 Subtotal		–	–	–	–		
		Educational Affordability Total (All Phases)		$400	$400	–	–		

STRENGTHENING WORKFORCE DEVELOPMENT

Developing a Palestinian workforce that is ready to compete in the global economy.

GOALS

Increase female labor force participation from 20 to 35 percent

Strengthening Workforce Development

Youth and Women

Science, Technology, Engineering, and Mathematics

Technical and Vocational Education

Internships and Apprenticeships

Workforce Training

STRENGTHENING WORKFORCE DEVELOPMENT

YOUTH AND WOMEN

US$ in mm unless otherwise specified)

	Project	Description	Phase	Total Est. Cost	Financing Grants	Financing Concessional Loans	Financing Private	Implementation Timeline
1	Career Counseling, Specialized Training, and Job Placement	Provide Palestinian youth and women with employer-focused training, career counseling, and job-placement services.	1	$10	$10	–	–	1 year; program to last 5 years
2	Technical Assistance for Creation of a Youth and Women Employment Initiative	Provide technical assistance for the Palestinian public sector to develop a comprehensive strategy to boost youth and women's employment.	1	10	10	–	–	2 Years
			Phase 1 Subtotal	$20	$20	–	–	
			Phase 2 Subtotal	–	–	–	–	
			Phase 3 Subtotal	–	–	–	–	
			Youth and Women Total (All Phases)	$20	$20	–	–	

STRENGTHENING WORKFORCE DEVELOPMENT

SCIENCE, TECHNOLOGY, ENGINEERING, AND MATHEMATICS

(US$ in mm unless otherwise is specified)

	Project	Description	Phase	Total Est. Cost	Financing Grants	Concessional Loans	Private	Implementation Timeline
1	Science, Technology, Engineering, and Mathematics (STEM) Commercial Partnerships	Sponsor research and development partnerships between Palestinian and international companies. Encourage international firms to partner with Palestinians in the development of new commercial technologies.	1	$50	$25	-	$25	4 Years
2	Science, Technology, Engineering, and Mathematics (STEM) Partnerships at Research Institutions	Sponsor educational training and research and development partnerships between Palestinian and global research institutions to focus on scientific research in STEM fields.	1	50	25	-	25	4 Years
			Phase 1 Subtotal	$100	$50	-	$50	
			Phase 2 Subtotal	-	-	-	-	
			Phase 3 Subtotal	-	-	-	-	
			Science, Technology, Engineering, and Mathematics Total (All Phases)	$100	$50	-	$50	

STRENGTHENING WORKFORCE DEVELOPMENT

TECHNICAL AND VOCATIONAL EDUCATION

US$ in mm unless otherwise specified

	Project	Description	Phase	Total Est. Cost	Financing			Implementation Timeline
					Grants	Concessional Loans	Private	
1	Technical and Vocational Training	Build the capacity of vocational institutions; work with educators to develop new curriculums to focus on high-demand areas such as healthcare, tourism, and ICT; partner with the private sector to support dual-vocational, work-study programs; and upgrade equipment and classrooms in vocational facilities.	1	$75	$40	–	$35	3 years
		Phase 1 Subtotal		$75	$40	–	$35	
		Phase 2 Subtotal		–	–	–	–	
		Phase 3 Subtotal		–	–	–	–	
		Technical and Vocational Education Total (All Phases)		$75	$40	–	$35	

STRENGTHENING WORKFORCE DEVELOPMENT

INTERNSHIPS AND APPRENTICESHIPS

(US$ in mm unless otherwise specified)

	Project	Description	Phase	Total Est. Cost	Financing			Implementation Timeline
					Grants	Concessional Loans	Private	
1	Internships	Develop new internship programs for Palestinian students, which may allow Palestinians the opportunity to work internationally.	1	$50	$25	–	$25	1 year; program to last 10 years
2	Apprenticeships	Provide grants to the private sector to encourage part-time apprenticeship programs for Palestinian secondary and post-graduate school students.	1	50	10	–	40	1 year; program to last 10 years
			Phase 1 Subtotal	$100	$35	–	$65	
			Phase 2 Subtotal	–	–	–	–	
			Phase 3 Subtotal	–	–	–	–	
		Internships and Apprenticeships Total (All Phases)		$1.10	$35	–	$65	

STRENGTHENING WORKFORCE DEVELOPMENT

WORKFORCE TRAINING

US$ in mm unless otherwise specified)

#	Project	Description	Phase	Total Est. Cost	Financing Grants	Concessional Loans	Private	Implementation Timeline
1	In-Service Training Programs	Provide financial incentives to the private sector to expand training programs and facilities to support Palestinian employees.	1	$25	$25	-	-	1 year; program to last 5 years
2	Re-taining Programs	Provide Palestinians in the workforce with opportunities to gain new skills and receive additional training at vocational institutions and other institutions.	1	25	25	-	-	1 year; program to last 5 years
		Phase 1 Subtotal		$50	$50	-	-	-
		Phase 2 Subtotal		-	-	-	-	-
		Phase 3 Subtotal		-	-	-	-	-
		Workforce Training Total (All Phases)		$50	$50	-	-	-

INVESTING IN HEALTHCARE

In proving healthcare quality and access, and increasing preventive healthcare services.

GOALS

Reduce infant mortality from 18 to 9 per 1,000 births

Increase average life expectancy from 74 to 80 years

Investing in Healthcare

Healthcare Access

Healthcare Quality

Preventive Healthcare

INVESTING IN HEALTH CARE

HEALTH CARE ACCESS

US$ in mm unless otherwise specified

	Project	Description	Phase	Total Est. Cost	Financing Grants	Concessional Loans	Private	Implementation Timeline
1	Providing Essential Medicines	Provide additional supplies of medicine in the West Bank and Gaza for Palestinians in need of care.	1	$50	$50	-	-	1 year
2	Mobile Clinics for Underserved Communities	Finance the development of new mobile clinics to provide primary care to underserved communities.	1	50	50	-	-	1 year
3	Upgrading Facilities and Equipment	Upgrade and secure new equipment for Palestinian hospitals and healthcare facilities, particularly to benefit patients in need of specialized treatments.	3	900	300	600	-	9 years
		Phase 1 Subtotal		$100	$100	-	-	
		Phase 2 Subtotal		-	-	-	-	
		Phase 3 Subtotal		900	300	600	-	
		Healthcare Access (All Phases)		$1,000	$400	$600	-	

INVESTING IN HEALTH CARE

HEALTH CARE QUALITY

US$ in mm unless otherwise specified)

	Project	Description	Phase	Total Est. Cost	Financing Grants	Concessional Loans	Private	Implementation Timeline
1	Hospital Standards Program	Build institutional capacity to inspect and enforce standards across the medical field.	1	$25	$25	–	–	2 years
2	Improving Efficiency of Services	Provide technical support to the relevant authorities to improve the delivery and efficiency of healthcare services, including opportunities to consolidate existing facilities and care centers.	1	20	20	–	–	3 years
3	Training for Medical Staff	Develop an in-service training program for medical professionals, including doctors, nurses, and administrators to improve professional skills and maintain the requisite standard of care for their patients.	1	75	75	–	–	2 years; program to last 5 years
	Phase 1 Subtotal			$120	$120	–	–	
	Phase 2 Subtotal			–	–	–	–	
	Phase 3 Subtotal			–	–	–	–	
	Healthcare Quality (All Phases)			$120	$120	–	–	

INVESTING IN HEALTH CARE

PREVENTIVE HEALTH CARE

US$ in mm unless otherwise specified)

Project	Description	Total Est. Cost	Phase	Financing Grants	Concessional Loans	Private	Implementation Timeline
1 Preventive Care and Public Awareness Programs	Invest in primary and secondary prevention programs, including measures to reduce tobacco use, encourage a healthy diet, and promote and facilitate regular physical activity.	1	$200				2 Years
	Phase 1 Subtotal		$200	$200	–	–	
	Phase 2 Subtotal		–	–	–	–	
	Phase 3 Subtotal		–	–	–	–	
	Preventive Healthcare Total (All Phases)		$200	$200	–	–	

IMPROVING QUALITY OF LIFE

Enhancing urban areas, recreational facilities, cultural institutions, and municipal services.

GOALS

Build a Palestinian Athletic Development Center

Construct a new Palestinian Cultural Center and Museum

Improving Quality of Life

Arts and Culture

Sports and Athletics

Municipal Services

ARTS AND CULTURE

US$ in mm unless otherwise specified

	Project	Description	Phase	Total Est. Cost	Financing Grants	Concessional Loans	Private	Implementation Timeline
1	Grants for the Arts	Provide grants to support talented Palestinian artists, musicians, and writers.	1	$80	$80	-	-	1 year; program to last five years
2	Palestinian Museum and Cultural Center	Construct a new cultural center and museum, with the potential for a modern theater where Palestinians and international artists can perform.	3	150	100	50	-	8 years
		Phase 1 Subtotal		$80	$80	-	-	
		Phase 2 Subtotal		-	-	-	-	
		Phase 3 Subtotal		150	100	50	-	
		Arts and Culture Total (All Phases)		$230	$180	$50	-	

IMPROVING QUALITY OF LIFE

SPORTS AND ATHLETICS

US$ in mm unless otherwise specified

	Project	Description	Phase	Total Est. Cost	Grants	Financing Concessional Loans	Private	Implementation Timeline
1	Youth Sports	Support and invest in youth sports across the West Bank and Gaza to increase participation and improve equipment and facilities.	1	$25	$25	–	–	2 years
2	Palestinian Athletic Development Center	Develop a new state-of-the-art athletic training center for Palestinians and provide opportunities to train at international facilities.	2	75	75	–	–	5 years
			Phase 1 Subtotal	$25	$25	–	–	
			Phase 2 Subtotal	75	75	–	–	
			Phase 3 Subtotal	–		–	–	
		Sports and Athletics Total (All Phases)		$100	$100	–	–	

IMPROVING QUALITY OF LIFE

MUNICIPAL SERVICES

(US$ in mm unless otherwise specified)

	Project	Description	Phase	Total Est. Cost	Financing Grants	Concessional Loans	Private	Implementation Timeline
1	Recreational Development	Develop new public parks, beach areas, and recreational centers.	1	$50	$50	-	-	4 years
2	Investing in Public Libraries and Community Centers	Invest in the construction of new community centers and libraries, as well as rehabilitate existing facilities to provide more services to the community.	1	50	50	-	-	3 years
3	Expanding Municipal Services and Infrastructure	Construct municipal infrastructure such as sidewalks, greenspaces, parks, and walkways in cities and towns; renovate public buildings and implement revitalization projects for urban areas.	1	200	200	-	-	4 years
			Phase 1 Subtotal	$300	$300	-	-	
			Phase 2 Subtotal	-	-	-	-	
			Phase 3 Subtotal	-	-	-	-	
			Municipal Services Total (All Phases)	$300	$300	-	-	

## CHAPTER THREE

ENHANCING PALESTINIAN GOVERNANCE

3
ENHANCING PALESTINIAN GOVERNANCE

Accountable & Agile Government

Empowered & Prosperous People

Thriving & Integrated Economy

Creating a Better Business Environment

Institution Building

Improving Government Operations

CREATING A BETTER BUSINESS ENVIRONMENT

Improving the legal and regulatory framework to support private-sector growth and create new economic opportunities.

GOALS

Achieve a World Bank Doing Business ranking of 75 or better

Complete a comprehensive database of land ownership

Creating a Better Business Environment

Property Rights

Legal and Tax Framework

Capital Markets and Monetary Policy

International Trade and Foreign Direct Investment

CREATING A BETTER BUSINESS ENVIRONMENT

PROPERTY RIGHTS

US$ in mm unless otherwise specified

	Project	Description	Phase	Total Est. Cost	Financing Grants	Concessional Loans	Private	Implementation Timeline
1	Property Ownership Resolution	Enhance court capacity to quickly and effectively resolve property disputes and contested ownership claims.	1	$60	$60	–	–	3 years; 50 percent within 1 year, the remainder within 3 years
2	Business Registration	Build an efficient, one-stop-shop for business registration and other resources for business owners.	1	50	50	–	–	1 year
3	Land Registration Database	Work with the Palestinian public sector and the private sector to ensure land ownership is effectively registered in a comprehensive database.	2	30	30	–	–	5 years
			Phase 1 Subtotal	$110	$110	–	–	
			Phase 2 Subtotal	30	30	–	–	
			Phase 3 Subtotal	–	–	–	–	
			Property Rights Total (All Phases)	$140	$140	–	–	

CREATING A BETTER BUSINESS ENVIRONMENT

LEGAL AND TAX FRAMEWORK

US$ in mm unless otherwise specified

Project	Description	Phase	Total Est. Cost	Financing Grants	Concessional Loans	Private	Implementation Timeline
1 New Laws and Reforms	Provide technical assistance to streamline regulations across all sectors to excite economic growth. Some priorities may include (but will not be limited to) the implementation of commercial, competition, investment promotion, intellectual property, and public-private partnership laws, with emphasis on the implementation of an efficient and low-burden tax system.	1	$50	$50	–	–	3 years
		Phase 1 Subtotal	$50	$50	–	–	
		Phase 2 Subtotal	–	–	–	–	
		Phase 3 Subtotal	–	–	–	–	
		Legal and Tax Framework Total (All Phases)	$50	$50	–	–	

CREATING A BETTER BUSINESS ENVIRONMENT

CAPITAL MARKETS AND MONETARY POLICY

US$ in mm unless otherwise specified)

	Project	Description	Phase	Total Est. Cost	Total Grants	Financing Concessional Loans	Financing Private	Implementation Timeline
1	Technical Assistance for the Financial Sector and Regulators	Provide technical assistance for Palestinian financial institutions and the Palestinian financial sector to support best lending practices and appropriately expand access to capital for underserved sectors and demographics.	1	$25	$25	–	–	2 Years
		Phase 1 Subtotal		$25	$25	–	–	
		Phase 2 Subtotal		–	–	–	–	
		Phase 3 Subtotal		–	–	–	–	
		Capital Markets and Monetary Policy Total (All Phases)		$25	$25	–	–	

CREATING A BETTER BUSINESS ENVIRONMENT

INTERNATIONAL TRADE AND FOREIGN DIRECT INVESTMENT

(US$ in mm unless otherwise specified)

	Project	Description	Phase	Total Est. Cost	Financing Grants	Concessional Loans	Private	Implementation Timeline
1	Technical Support for Customs/Trade Functions	Provide training to build the capacity of the Palestinian public sector to manage crossing points, inspect goods, and facilitate trade.	1	$50	$50	-	-	2 years
2	Technical Support to Develop Palestinian Trade Policy	Provide technical support to the Palestinian public sector to develop a new trade regime and framework that facilitates growth in exports and foreign direct investment.	1	25	25	-	-	2 years
			Phase 1 Subtotal	$75	$75	-	-	
			Phase 2 Subtotal	-	-	-	-	
			Phase 3 Subtotal	-	-	-	-	
			International Trade and Foreign Direct Investment Total (All Phases)	$75	$75	-	-	

INSTITUTION BUILDING

Implementing systems and policies that ensure government transparency and accountability to the people.

GOALS

Improve government transparency, with a Transparency International Corruption Perceptions Index score of 60 or better

Implement an e-government system, achieving a United Nations E-Government Development Index score greater than 0.75

Institution Building

Judicial Independence

Accountability

Transparency

Civil Society

INSTITUTION BUILDING

JUDICIAL INDEPENDENCE

US$ in mm unless otherwise ie specified)

	Project	Description	Phase	Total Est. Cost	Financing Grants	Concessional Loans	Private	Implementation Timeline
1	Court Filing System s Autom ation	Provide technical support to stream line and m odernize court processes. This w ill include developing electronic filing procedures and databases to store, organize, and search court records.	1	$25	$25	–	–	3 years
2	Court Capacity and Training	Provide technical assistance to build the capacity of the court system to enforce contract law, address charges of corruption, and un law fulgovernm ent actions.	1	50	50	–	–	1 year program to last 5 years
3	Supporting Independent Judicial Institutions	Im plem ent reform s that protect the independence of the judiciary and protect court w orkers from retaliation.	1	50	50	–	–	2 years
4	Alternative D ispute Resolution and Arb itration	Invest in increased capacity to provide alternative dispute resolution m echanism s.	2	50	50	–	–	5 years
		Phase 1 Subtotal		$125	$125	–	–	
		Phase 2 Subtotal		50	50	–	–	
		Phase 3 Subtotal		–	–	–	–	
		Judicial Independence Total (All Phases)		$175	$175	–	–	

INSTITUTION BUILDING

ACCOUNTABILITY

US$ in mn unless otherwise specified

#	Project	Description	Phase	Total Est. Cost	Financing			Implementation Timeline
					Grants	Concessional Loans	Private	
1	Enhancing Anti-Corruption Bodies	Provide technical assistance and training to build the capacity of the anti-corruption authorities.	1	$25	$25	–	–	3 years
2	Improving Internal Auditing Capabilities	Develop the capacity to audit public-sector expenditures and conduct investigations.	1	25	25	–	–	3 years
3	Institutional Reforms	Provide technical support to develop standardized and transparent processes and procedures for human and resources and regulatory reviews, in areas such as license issuance.	1	25	25	–	–	3 years
		Phase 1 Subtotal		$75	$75	–	–	
		Phase 2 Subtotal		–	–	–	–	
		Phase 3 Subtotal		–	–	–	–	
		Accountability Total (All Phases)		$75	$75	–	–	

INSTITUTION BUILDING

TRANSPARENCY

US$ in mm unless otherwise specified)

Project	Description	Phase	Total Est. Cost	Financing			Implementation Timeline
				Grants	Concessional Loans	Private	
1 Improving Access to Information	Develop a transparent system for public reporting of public-sector decisions, particularly with regard to procurement, contracts, licenses, and hiring. As part of this system, citizens will also be able to request information from public-sector institutions on decisions and policies. This initiative will be coupled with the e-governance project.	1	$50	$50	–	–	3 years
		Phase 1 Subtotal	$50	$50	–	–	
		Phase 2 Subtotal	–	–	–	–	
		Phase 3 Subtotal	–	–	–	–	
		Transparency Total (All Phases)	$50	$50	–	–	

INSTITUTION BUILDING

CIVIL SOCIETY

(US$ in mm unless otherwise specified)

Project	Description	Phase	Total Est. Cost	Financing Grants	Concessional Loans	Private	Implementation Timeline
1 Protecting Journalists and Civil Society	Support independent organizations capable of investigating claims of abuse or intimidation of journalists and NGO workers.	1	$30	$30	-	-	1 year
2 Supporting Independent Civil Society Groups	Provide grants to advocacy organizations and civil society groups that focus on transparency and accountability.	1	150	150	-	-	1 year; program to last 10 years
		Phase 1 Subtotal	$180	$180	-	-	
		Phase 2 Subtotal	-	-	-	-	
		Phase 3 Subtotal	-	-	-	-	
		Civil Society Total (All Phases)	$180	$180	-	-	

IMPROVING GOVERNMENT OPERATIONS

Enhancing government services through civil service training and ensuring a sustainable public-sector budget.

GOALS

Pass a sustainable Palestinian public-sector budget

Improving Government Operations

Fiscal Sustainability

Civil Service

Service Delivery

FISCAL SUSTAINABILITY

US$ in mm unless otherwise specified

#	Project	Description	Phase	Est. Cost	Total Grants	Financing Concessional Loans	Private	Implementation Timeline
1	Arrears Payments / Operations & Maintenance Contingency Reserve	Provide payment of arrears to local vendors and create an operations and maintenance contingency reserve to support key infrastructure projects.	1	$1,750	$1,000	$750	-	6 months: program to last 5 years
2	Increasing Revenue Collection Efficiency	Invest in new systems that will allow the Palestinians to manage and monitor the collection of revenues at commercial crossing points, with an emphasis on the implementation of anti-corruption safeguards.	1	25	25	-	-	3 years
3	Managing Expenditures	Provide technical assistance to help the Palestinians to evaluate expenditures and budgetary processes and identify potential efficiencies, with an emphasis on the implementation of anti-corruption safeguards.	1	25	25	-	-	3 years
4	Procurement Management	Standardize efficient and accountable processes for Palestinian public-sector procurement decisions, with an emphasis on the implementation of anti-corruption safeguards.	1	25	25	-	-	3 years
		Phase 1 Subtotal		$1,825	$1,075	$750	-	
		Phase 2 Subtotal		-	-	-	-	
		Phase 3 Subtotal		-	-	-	-	
		Fiscal Sustainability Total (All Phases)		$1,825	$1,075	$750	-	

IMPROVING GOVERNMENT OPERATIONS

CIVIL SERVICE

(US$ in mm unless otherwise specified)

#	Project	Description	Phase	Total Est. Cost	Financing			Implementation Timeline
					Grants	Concessional Loans	Private	
1	Civil Service Training and Certifications	Support the development of a civil service training program to provide educational opportunities for public-sector employees.	1	$50	$50	-	-	3 years
2	Streamlining Civil Service	Develop incentives for civil servants to transition to the private sector while increasing salaries for top-performing civil servants through a merit-based standard. This will create new efficiencies, improve service delivery, and help ensure the Palestinian public sector is fiscally sustainable.	1	250	250	-	-	3 years
3	Attracting Global Expertise	Support the development of a team of experts— from the West Bank and Gaza and internationally— to work with the Palestinian public sector and rapidly scale up capacity and implement and manage new projects.	1	100	100	-	-	1 year; program to last 5 years
			Phase 1 Subtotal	$400	$400	-	-	
			Phase 2 Subtotal	-	-	-	-	
			Phase 3 Subtotal	-	-	-	-	
			Civil Service Total (All Phases)	$400	$400	-	-	

SERVICE DELIVERY

US$ in mm unless otherwise specified)

	Project	Description	Phase	Total Est. Cost	Financing			Implementation Timeline
					Grants	Concessional Loans	Private	
1	Public-Private Partnerships	Identify services and utilities that could be provided by the private sector to improve efficiency and reduce costs, particularly in areas of service delivery such as electricity, transportation, and telecommunications.	1	$35	$35	-	-	3 years
2	Palestinian E-Governance	Implement a system to expand the scope of online public-sector services, including payment services, job searches, passport requests, and commercial registration.	2	300	300	-	-	5 years
		Phase 1 Subtotal		$35	$35	-	-	
		Phase 2 Subtotal		300	300	-	-	
		Phase 3 Subtotal		-	-	-	-	
		Service Delivery Total (All Phases)		$335	$335	-	-	

CONCLUSION

While the vision is ambitious, it is achievable. The future of the Palestinians is one of huge promise and potential. The Palestinian story does not end here. Their story is just being written.

9 787966 208602